MW00943198

Everything Changed -

The ViệtNam War and American Culture

Lessons Not Learned

~~~

3rd Ed

Heyward H. Macdonald, D.Min.
~Charlottesville, Virginia

*Sing to me, Muse, and through me tell the story
of that man skilled in all ways of contending,
the wanderer, harried for years on end,
after he plundered the stronghold
on the proud height of Troy…*

Homer
The Odyssey, Prologue

ISBN   9781512371048

© February, 2015
Heyward H. Macdonald

Create Space
U.S.A.

Mỹ Sơn

Southwest of DaNang, near the village of DuyPhú and the Lao border there is a large site of temples of the Champa Kingdom. It is the oldest archaeological site in Indochina and illustrates that early cultural influence of the South came from the Hindu peoples to the west and not the Chinese from the north. This photo was taken by me in March of 1999.

The photo on the cover, which I took earlier the same month, is of a traditional boat for a hamlet or family on one of the dragons (outlets) of the MeKong River near CanTho.

Vietnam or VietNam?

When this book was first published, I received two e-mails from Vietnamese Americans challenging my spelling of the name of their country of origin. I paid attention, and it does seem correct, since the name Viet Nam means "Southern Man". That is two concepts, though such is not definitive with other languages. Nevertheless, I have followed herein the convention they suggested by spelling the name of the country and usually places within it as two one syllable proper names, or "VietNam." This is unusual to us, but corresponds to the belief of many that the language is mostly monosyllabic, and that the name therefore might better be spelled in that way.

Forward

This small book is an outgrowth of a course and a 90 minute lecture I was asked to deliver for the Osher Institute at the University of Virginia in 2014. That means that this one-time soldier has had a lot of time since the ViệtNam War to think, not so much about my experiences, but rather that of the Nation. My graduate work as well as some small work with veterans of that war have all contributed; yet, I offer this with some apology, since I consider everything I have to tell you to be very superficial and naïve – not because I haven't read tens of thousands of pages on the subject; but rather because the subject is controversial, bewildering in its complexity, and beyond my limited resources and intellect. There is also lying in wait the difficulty to me as a Westerner of understanding a culture very different from our own; but, that is the challenge always before us in formulating or evaluating any foreign policy.

Nevertheless, I shall try to serve you as best I can. I shall try to stay on the topic of how the war was both daughter and mother to our culture, and what questions compel our attention now. Herein, I shall try to stress Culture and Public Policy, along with quite a lot of important, supportive history.

I consider ViệtNam to be the "Elephant in the Room" of our time. This country sent our youth halfway across the planet to engage in a nasty, violent war;

but, when it didn't turn out the way we wanted, we as a people, for many reasons, tried very hard to forget.

But the elephant, I am told, does NOT forget; and, in fact, that elephant lives in our gut to this day, and needs to be brought out and examined. Our culture was profoundly changed by this experience, I think more so than by recent wars; and it is important to understand how and why. Unfortunately, major lessons that could have been incorporated into our public debate and policy were missed, and some appropriate change has not yet happened.

It is also true that, in addition to having been a very different culture from the West, that of the Vietnamese people was also drastically changed by this watershed in their history. It is now an emerging nation, which we have recognized officially, and with which we shall have to live as a member of the family of nations. The need to understand is still there. The need to understand other cultures is always there.

Loren Baritz, a cultural historian, writes, "A child can learn by touching a flame, can a nation?"[1] That is the question that disturbs my sleep, for we are a people with many matches and not much instruction in their use – and much on their misuse. Furthermore, how does a democracy make such corporate judgments? A dictatorship can do so at the whim of the leader. In our system, each citizen has her or his own opinion,

---

[1] Baritz, Loren. <u>Backfire: A History of How American Culture Led Us Into VietNam and Made Us Fight the Way We Did</u>, (William Morrow, NY, 1985) P. 11.

or chooses by default to have no opinion whatever. Perhaps reading this will provoke some memory, some informed dialogue, some passion. Maybe we will become citizens and not subjects once again.

There is an Elephant in the room, and here is how I plan to deal with its presence. Please remember, I don't object to your having opposing beliefs and conclusions. I understand and am sad that my book might cause pain for some who lost family members or soldiers who lost their youth and vitality in that war. These people, as would I, would love to have our sacrifice validated by meaning and justice, but that is hard to find. My objective, rather, is to encourage thoughtful dialogue on issues of war, such as when and how we fight and who decides, so that such sacrifice might not be made unwisely in the future. First, however, allow me to say thanks.

I owe a much-belated thanks to my guys who worked for me in ViệtNam. I was their Lieutenant for a year, first at Ft. Lewis, and then in PhuLoi and like places and they served very well; but, I was moved to Battalion Staff for my last months in-country and subsequently left without thanking them, and that has bothered me ever since.

So, now, I never fail to thank a veteran of whatever war, of whatever rank, and of whatever era, and beg you to do the same.

Table of Contents

Part I: The Awakening of Memory

You know a Soldier or Marine who served in the VietNam War – or maybe several. Pick one and think about him. What has he told you – probably not much. What did he do – you probably don't know. What are his deepest thoughts – you likely have no idea. We are like that for lots of reasons, some of which are listed in this book.[2]

Do you remember when he returned from the War; or, have you heard stories? Do you know what the country was like to which he returned? Perhaps our society has forgotten. I can promise you he has not. For him, and for families of warriors who did not return alive or were horribly wounded in body, mind, or spirit, everything changed.

Perhaps there are some veterans of that war reading this book. I pause and say to you, "Welcome home my brother."

And, what do you know of the Vietnamese people and their culture? What did we ever know, for that matter? This is important too, and a central point of this book.

---

[2] Note the masculine pronoun. The war in VietNam was our last all-male war. We had nurses in the three major base camps, and they served magnificently and with great dedication and self-sacrifice, but the war was carried on entirely by men.

It was a half-century ago. I had a high school student ask me in class recently if the VietNam War was before or after the Civil War. They have no idea, so how can they incorporate the lessons from that war in deliberations regarding conflicts in their future? Therefore, I want to turn back the clock to remind all of us what those tumultuous years were like, lest we, too, forget. If we forget, or fail to pass on what we know, the nation will be much the poorer, and the danger far greater. If you are of a more recent generation, that is all right too. Think on these things.

Video of the Mind

So, think about the soldier you picked above or talk to an old soldier and see what he says. Let the cares of today drift away. Alternatively, recall those days as it might have been for you in a television newscast of the period – perhaps Walter Cronkite. Allow that video to play across your mind. This is important, so come back in about five minutes. No, seriously, folks: take the time to settle down and let these memories return. We will deal with them in this little book. It is about remembering.

++++++++++++++++++++++++++++++++++++++

OK, welcome back.

Now, turn the page and slowly and contemplatively work through the next paragraphs.

What did you see about your soldier or hear in your newscast?

Did you find your soldier on a jungle trail or in cantonment after an exhausting few days in the bush? What did you see? Was he watchful? Was he exhausted? What did you see in his eyes?

Did you see his youth? His Vulnerability? His Fear? If your soldier was in base camp, did you hear any of the music spawned by the war? What titles do you remember?

Did you perceive the despair of ever getting home? The Nihilism? The extreme violence? The inversion of the moral and religious order at an age of incompletely-formed moral sense?

Or did you notice in your newscast the use of our big weapons: the dehumanization of the Vietnamese: the loss and maiming of children; the clash of cultures?

Do you remember the civil unrest that tore our country apart: the rioting, the burning cities: the horrid assassinations?

Do you recall the sadness and the tears?

Perhaps it brought back memories of your own service? Did you leave buddies behind? If you were a family member, did you have a loved one who did not return?

17

Do you remember how we got into that war? Have you thought about the real nature of it?

What, really, do you know of the ancient Vietnamese culture?

Subsequent generations have little idea of these things. We need to tell them.

The Price of Not Remembering

We are going to think about all these things in this short book, because if we fail to remember and fail to think critically about history we will make the same horrid mistakes again – in fact, in my opinion, have done so regularly. George Santayana did say, "Those who cannot remember the past are condemned to repeat it."[3]

So, that is why I am writing this – not to tell war stories, there are many with far better ones than mine – rather I am here to encourage us all to process our national memory, and maybe come together as a people to make things good and decent and hopeful in the future.

---

[3] George Santayana. Reason in Common Sense, The Life of Reason, Vol 1, Chapter 12 "Flux and Constancy in Human Nature." Dover Publications, 1980.

Part II: Our Culture and the Path to War

Right up front I want to say that I believe the United States to be the greatest, most generous, most free nation that has ever graced this planet. I, like most veterans in any number of surveys, would pick up arms again if our country were directly threatened.

Here is a representative piece of history that is illustrative of why we feel that way:

Pride in Our Country

Simon Wiesenthal, the famed Nazi Hunter, gave a video interview, which I have seen several times. The last time I saw it, I wrote down what he said.

He spoke of his confinement in concentration camps from 1941 until May of 1945 when General George Patton's 3rd Army liberated the camp at Mauthausen, Austria.

He described the moment he heard the American Soldiers arrive.

> I ... looked up to see the most beautiful sight I have ever seen. It was the American Flag on the lead tank. I saw every star on that blue field; there was the Star of Justice, and the Star of Friendship, and the Star of

Culture. And I saw the Stripes, each representing a road to Freedom.[4]

Whenever I hear of such, I feel very proud of my country. That is good; it is patriotic; it celebrates the principles on which this country was founded and by which on our best days we try to live. Our hearts sing at this and other powerful quotations of our Founders, such as Thomas Paine's words:

The Sun never shined on a cause of greater worth,

and,

We have it in our power to begin the world over again.

This perceived identity is, however, part of our developing national self-image that led us to VietNam.

There is more, of course:

- The particular belief of our founders that the United States was leading the way in rule by the people

- The powerful language of Thomas Jefferson such as the "Declaration of Independence" and James Madison and the Constitution of the United States

- There was the "Monroe Doctrine," by which we proclaimed suzerainty over our hemisphere

---

[4] Kennedy, Ludovic. "Ludovic Kennedy Meets Nazi-Hunter Simon Wiesenthal", B.B.C 2, first aired 20 November 1989.

- What came to be known as "Manifest Destiny," by which we were determined to spread the special virtues of European America and our institutions to the rest of the continent

- The "Four Freedoms" of Franklin D. Roosevelt[5]

- And so forth.

These are all part of our National Mythology, and this mythology can be determinative. Here is how.

A National Mythology

Loren Baritz writes in his study, <u>Backfire</u>, that there were cultural forces afoot in this country and an historical context that made the VietNam War inevitable.[6] I hate to think that; but, lets have a look at that hypothesis.

In the Sermon on the Mount (in <u>Matthew</u> 5), Jesus says, "You are the Light of the World, a City that is set upon a Hill cannot be hidden." Politicians have made

---

[5] Roosevelt, Franklin D. Address to Congress of 6 January 1941, insisting that the whole world deserved the foundational beliefs of the United States of America, including freedom from Fear, freedom of speech, freedom of religion, and freedom from want. These resonated with the Congress, and lead eventually to the "Lend Lease" program to help our allies, but interestingly would not fly with many peoples of the world today.

[6] Baritz. P. 321.

much of this statement in proclaiming a special, godly mission for the United States of America. This translation of a spiritual destiny into a temporal, nationalistic one is problematic.

The first to use it was John Winthrop, who admonished his Massachusetts Bay Colonists on the deck of Arbella that they were to become "a City upon a Hill, setting an example of charity, affection, and unity to the world," and that God would, "hold them in judgment if they did not."

This feeling of a special, godly status for the United States seems to have been pervasive even before we became a world power. Herman Melville writes in the mid-19th century that "We Americans are the particular, chosen People - the Israel of our time, we bear the Ark of the liberties of the world." [7]

This use of sacred text was repeated by John Kennedy when he advanced the concept of "American Exceptionalism," and said that it was our, "God-given right and obligation to provide the moral leadership for this planet."

And, Ronald Regan, "The Great Communicator," used it many times, saying, "I have spoken of the Shining City all my life." He equated the United States with the Promised Land, and said, "You and I have a rendezvous with destiny. We will preserve for our children this, the last best hope of man on earth,

---

[7] Herman Melville. White Jacket: or The World in a Man-of-War, Harper and Brothers, 1850. Ch. 36.

or we will sentence them to take the last step into a thousand years of darkness."[8]

John Kennedy told a joke on himself once that holds a kernel of truth about those who aspire to high office. He said, "Several nights ago, I dreamed that the good Lord touched me on the shoulder and said, 'Don't worry, you'll be the Democratic Presidential Nominee in 1960. What's more, you'll be elected. I told [U.S. Senator] Stu Symington about my dream. 'Funny thing,' he said, 'I had the same dream myself.' We both told our dreams to Lyndon Johnson, and Johnson said, 'That's funny. For the life of me, I can't remember tapping either one of you two boys for the job."[9]

That is heady stuff!   Perhaps there is a certain amount of messianic self-view needed to desire the Presidency.   Perhaps that also is part of the willingness shown by our presidents to go to war.

It can be said, however, that Kennedy and Reagan were providing an ideology for their time, and were exhibiting leadership thereby; but, in conjunction with our formational mythology, storied performance in World War II, and our rapidly increasing wealth, they gave us a sense of superiority and destiny much like that of Rome at its zenith.

---

[8] Ronald Reagan. "A Time for Choosing", Speech delivered on behalf of Barry Goldwater's 1964 presidential campaign, 27 Oct 1964.

We could out-produce, out think, out-manage, out spend, and out-fight any other people in the world. And we were proud of it. I know I was. In part, I still am.

In addition, it was all wrapped up in religious confusion in what at the time was perceived as a people of European, Judeo-Christian origin.

William Mahedy, author of Out of the Night, calls this "American Civil Religion", saying that it played no small part in our experience in VietNam, and its effect on our veterans. It seems to me that when our congregations sang, "Onward Christian Soldiers" in the 50's we took it quite literally. We seemed to think God would always give us the victory and not allow our soldiers to die when fighting in a "godless land".[10]

We had come to believe that our way of life, our economy, and our political system were God-given tools by which other peoples of whatever culture could be free and lead rewarding lives. The whole world wanted to be like us, or so we thought.

We had a distinct National Mythology, and in certitude of our own righteousness didn't understand any other culture, or even try; and every nation goes to war out of its leaders' and its people's understanding of its national mythology.

---

[10] William Mahedy. Out of the Night, Ballantine Books, 1986 or Radix Press, 2004, P. 20.

Lt. General Phillip B. Davidson was General Westmoreland's J-2 (Intelligence) at MACV in the middle of the war. He calls this propensity to see things only our way, "Ethnocentrism". He says it is the "Grand dragon, awaiting all commanders – a bias toward one's own culture and a distortion of that of other nations." Further, he says that, "'EC' is a distortion of reality, and truly a deadly sin. – It was so common in VietNam that no one recognized it."

Davidson reports that Johnson used to interview himself about what he would do if he were Ho Chi Minh and send off directives accordingly, later to find that Ho didn't share his opinion.[11]

Because of this, our people and our leaders, both political and military, made the assumption that the peasants of VietNam would welcome us with open arms as their liberators, as had the people in France and Belgium, but those people were, after all, very much like us. The people of VietNam were not.

We found instead, sullen women, sitting by the trail chewing betel nut, and counting our soldiers as they passed by.

There is more to this, however. Not only does our National Mythology tell us that our way is the only way, but that the export of our way justifies whatever means we might employ. The problem of this "ends justifying the means" issue is that a nation is great not

[11] Davidson, Phillip B.. <u>Secrets of the VietNam War</u>, Prisidion Press, CA. 1990. P. 109.

for what it accomplishes, but for the principles for which it stands.

Our Predilection to Violence

Our nation was formed from a European culture that was steeped in the pre-Copernican views of Judeo-Christian Holy Writ and the teachings of the ancient church.   Until the advent of the scholarship of biblical form criticism and interpretation, people accepted the words of the Bible at face value without any understanding of context or human development. Some still do. Before you get a little upset at me, allow me to explain. Then you will really be upset.

The stories of the Bible were told and then written long before the Age of Enlightenment. They were an art form different from today's far more technical understanding of communication.   It is not unfair to consider the old stories sacred poetry, in that they tell of eternal truths far beyond the story line or the words used in it. In fact, they are capable, as sacred poetry, of conveying far deeper truths than can readily be done with our modern, technical language.

To say that Methuselah lived for 969 years is to say that he was a very old and wise man.[12]   Few could count beyond 20, so what did it matter – the point was not the years, but the wisdom and even more, the favor he found before God. To say that Jesus walked on water, coming to the disciples over the raging

---

[12] Genesis 5:27

surface of Lake Galilee is to say that if you are being tossed about in fear of your life on the waves of primeval chaos, you will be very comforted to know that Jesus can trample that chaos under his feet and join you in the little boat of human community, and everything will be all right.[13]

We read these stories and think, "Well that is just not true." It might very well be true to the teller and hearers of the story in that day, and for them and us the truth being told might be something other than the words might seem to say. To understand the Bible, we have to think like a pre-Copernican, pre-Enlightenment reader.

These stories were told and written in a very different language, culture, and time. The stories of the Jewish Scriptures, or what the Christians call the "Old Testament," was especially full of pronouncements and laws that were necessary from time to time to govern semi-nomadic, tribal, pre-state peoples. In that early time in written history, these tribes relied on themselves for some kind of justice.

If someone put out your eye or knocked out a tooth, you or your family would most likely put out both his eyes or knock out all the teeth of the perpetrator. The other village would then come kill a few of you and you would burn their village. The wisdom of the saying, "An eye for an eye; a tooth for a tooth,"[14] now is apparent. It does not say the eye or the tooth must

---

[13] Mark 6:45-56; Matthew 14:22-63; John 6:16-21
[14] Exodus 21:23-25

be taken, but rather that if retributive justice (the only kind then available) was employed, it should be limited to that specific act and not allowed to escalate. Jesus had something quite striking to say regarding this saying: "You have heard that it was said, 'Eye for eye, and tooth for tooth,' but I tell you, do not resist an evil person. If anyone slaps you on the right cheek, turn to them the other cheek also."[15]

Another clear example is the enthusiastic use of the death penalty in this country. Most of the civilized nations of the world will not extradite a person accused of a capital crime to the United States because of their view of the death penalty.[16] There is a clear trend among counties of the world to abolish the death penalty. Fifty years ago, there were no countries without capital punishment. Forty-six countries had abolished it by 1986 and by 2002 that

---

[15] Matthew 5:38

[16] Amnesty International, United States of America: The Death Penalty (appendix 12), 1987 and "Facts and Figures on the Death Penalty".
(The list of those countries who do not extradite capitol offenders to the U.S. is quite long, and includes all the European Countries except Belarus and even some of our closest allies, such as all members of the former British Commonwealth (Australia, Canada, New Zealand, South Africa, etc.) Other countries don't have any extradition treaty with us and so don't respond, including Russia, which no longer has a death penalty, and China, which does. Also, note the evolution of the understanding of Human Rights as expressed by, among other organizations, The Death Penalty Information Center. Richard C. Dieter, Executive Director.

number had risen to 111.[17] This penalty is usually defended in this country, most especially from the Christian literalist camp, by reference to the Old Testament. The New Testament certainly tells a different story, but the older tales and laws predominate in the debate, because they seem to vindicate our predilection to anger and vengeance .

Again, one must consider that in the times to which we refer, there were few police or judges (of the kind about which we speak here), and few, if any, facilities with which to isolate violent offenders from the communities they threatened. Semi-nomadic people don't carry prisons with them as they move around the land. The only way to protect the people was to put offenders to death. Such is not now the case.

We have lots of prisons and lots of police. The situation has changed, and the teachings of Jesus tell a far different story. Remember that he said to a woman, who under the law should have been stoned to death, "Go therefore and sin no more."[18] That is hardly retributive justice. Something in the human heart cries out to kill the person who injured us, but to be fully human, we must not. Capital Punishment destroys the humanity of the culture which practices it and the individuals who call for it.

---

[17] Hood, Roger. The Death Penalty: A World-wide Perspective, 1996. various. Also, Schabas, The Abolition of the Death Penalty in International Law, 1997.
[18] John 8:11

Furthermore, if one were to follow all those edicts from the Old Testament, our population would be much reduced. A study of the myriad of laws that fill the old texts include, for instance, death for "Boiling a goat in its mother's milk".[19]   So much for cream sauces.   Death is also prescribed for urinating in public.[20]   I don't do that, but the punishment seems extreme. The old edicts seem to give simple answers rather than teaching the more difficult work of becoming truly human, which is what is called for in what Christians call the New Testament.

It is true that absolute laws are attractive. Life lived in uncertainty is difficult. We are creatures who like to see things in terms of either good or evil. People different from us, then, have to be evil; people just like us must, by definition, be good.

Growth is difficult. It is much easier to quote a law and cut off debate. Our forbearers, not having the linguistic,   historical,   theological,   ethical,   or

---

[19] Exodus 23:19; Deuteronomy 14:21. Note that this prohibition refers to banning a ritual of a competing religious tradition that the Jewish People found threatening.
[20] I Samuel 25:22, 34; I Kings 14:10, 16:11, 21:21; 2 Kings 9:8. Note, though, that most translations read, "cut off" rather than execute, and peeing against the wall (in public) will send people running even today. This brings up the understanding that being cut off from the ancient community was considered a form of death. What other references to capital punishment in the Old Testament do you suppose mean the same thing? Note also that there were in Judaism traditions and rites of re-entry into the community – undoing death, so to speak.

philosophical tools or will to question this attitude, inherited a mindset that has at its core violence as a solution to human problems. This allowed the pilgrim fathers, for instance, to use ducking stools against their women and the various states to enact retributive laws that prescribe violence as a punishment.

Our culture perpetuates our mythology by passing it to our children. I grew up with the family gathered around the radio in the evenings listening to Gene Autry. WWII films, often starring John Wayne, were ever popular. We ran home from wherever we were to watch Roy Rogers shoot at the bad guys without ever bringing a drop of blood. Violence was clean and tidy. Death was temporary, or only applied to others. Bad guys were those in black hats. We played "Cowboys and Indians" by the day in the summertime. Indians were redskins and stereotyped as less capable, less well armed, really sneaky, and always were to lose the fights. It is not accidental that in VietNam at night we looked out through the concertina wire toward areas we couldn't control and called it "Indian Country".

The genre of the "Western" was born as the land was being settled by people of European origin. We spoke of Columbus "discovering" America, though the millions of people who lived here at the time knew very well that it was here. Horace Greely prophesied the western movement and encouraged it saying, "Go West young man."[21] The westward movement saga

---

[21] This phrase was related to the concept of "Manifest

spawned the mythology of the frontier, wherein it was taught to us that a real man lived by hunting his own game and carrying a big pistol on his hip to take care of snakes, Indians, and bandits (usually from Mexico). The vast land was there for the taking, and we took it. It became irrelevant that very few people in the West walked around with pistols on their hips. The stage was set for marginalization and demonization of anyone who looked different from us and got in our way. Violence was passed on as a tool of achieving national and personal goals.

A large issue for us today is gun control. A few people even in my quiet college town assert what is perceived as their 2nd Amendment Right to walk into a store with pistols on their hips, or even once, at the local Kroger store, an AR-15 slung on his shoulder. I spent a month with friends and family in South Australia recently and found universal disbelief that anyone in the U.S. thought bearing arms as a private citizen to be an acceptable idea or even that it deserves a national debate. My wife was asked if she carried a gun around our town.

Some of our staunchest allies are beginning to wonder about us. As for me, there was a time when I felt stripped naked without a firearm, but that was in VietNam, long ago. I left that far behind. For me, the

Destiny" and appeared first in the "Terre Haute Express" by John Soule in 1851. He said "Go west young man, and grow up with the country." Greeley favored westward expansion and used this phrase 14 years later and it caught on. He, therefore, wrongly, was credited for its origin.

question is more, how much new power do we want to give the Federal Government after 9-11. That could be an important component of the issue. We will talk more about distrust of the government in this book, since such is partly an outcome of the VietNam days.

Look today at what we watch on Television. How many of these shows portray violence and murder? It is true that most end with the "good guys" winning, but there is still a drenching with violence and death, day in and day out, that inures us to blood and dying, as long as it is the other person bleeding. I saw a new TV show advertised recently titled, "American Crime". Wonderful. I have traveled in dozens of countries, and many of the folks with whom I have spoken think of Hollywood productions and U.S. Television as accurate portrayals of our culture. Maybe that is true: our public policy seems to corroborate that allegation for them. This has been going on so long that it seems "hard wired". Can we really change?

This mindset, I contend, is what allows us to contemplate violence as an acceptable substitute for diplomacy. The people of VietNam were kind of in the way between us and our perceived enemy, they looked different from us, and had religious, political, and economic practices that looked strange to us, so our people were not overly disturbed when we descended on that country with extreme violence. It is just part of our culture. We need to work on that.

Geography and Public Policy

We in the United States seem to be puzzled when our European Allies from World War II balk when we ask them to join us in armed intervention far from our shores. They call for us to negotiate rather than threaten. Our belief is that negotiation is a sign of weakness, and that conviction seems supported by attempts in Europe to placate Hitler and his generals. The archetypical example, we point out, is the trip to Munich in 1938 of British Prime Minister Neville Chamberlain. He traded away the freedom of Poland for a vague guarantee from Hitler that he would not ask for more, and returned to England proclaiming, "Peace for Our Time." That didn't last long.

The French and Germans as well as the British have all been reluctant to approve of our military adventures since that War. Part of the reason is the mindset of being a new, pioneer nation carved out of a vast, thinly-settled continent. Part also is our geographical position in the world with two wide oceans protecting our flanks. Most people of the world, and certainly Europe, have a long history of living beside neighbors who could be a danger to them. They have had wars fought over their homelands more times than I have ever discovered. They have been devastated again and again, and have learned the pain of war and fear it greatly. They have developed through necessity and experience the attitude of negotiation to the point we would call "appeasement." We have not experienced war on our continent since the Civil War, though negotiation certainly did not happen then.

Since that war, we have felt protected by our geography, and in conjunction with our certitude in our foundational mythology, are less willing to be flexible, and less experienced in the art of negotiation. Remember that we are fairly unique in the history of nations in that we were formed by an idea and not just for the expansion of power or wealth. This idea is not for us negotiable; and therefore we, as a people, find ourselves alone in the world behind our oceans. We project our force and manipulate nations with our wealth, so are seen as arrogant and self-centered. We become the target for the disaffected of the world.

The Enlightenment in the West

Back in 1215 in England, King John was forced to agree to the adoption of the *Magna Carta*, by which it was proclaimed that the King was subject to, and not above, the Law. This legacy, though challenged from time to time, with our British roots and our settlement of a rich, bountiful land, along with our own revolution helped make us what we are. We are free, progressive people and proud of it.

The political thinking of the 18th Century, notably in France, gave people here a language of freedom to reject autocratic rule (although the French in their revolution soon thereafter substituted one autocracy for another). We are children of the Enlightenment, which was a particularly Western break from old patterns of philosophical thinking regarding science, theology, art, politics, and the freedom of the individual. Our subsequent success in nation-building led us to new belief in ourselves and our recently-discovered self-image, polity, and economy.

So, putting this chapter together, for the most part, we in the United States in the mid 20th Century thought of ourselves as a European-based (therefore superior), righteous, wealthy, innovative, youthful, pioneer culture; powerful winner of global wars; light on the hill and champion of freedom and democracy. Individualism, education, and achievement were highly honored. Time was linear with the future there for the making. The sky was the limit – even the moon. The social contract was driven by visions of creativity, progressive change, increased wealth, and improved life. Revolution was perceived as upsetting this wonderful progression.

Keep all this in mind as we look at the philosophy, polity, and traditions of the Sino-Vietnamese People, who were as far from us in thought as they were in distance – living as they did on the other side of the globe, and time.

Part III: Vietnamese Culture: The Inverse of Western Thought

It is hard for us in the West to put ourselves inside the mind of other peoples. I hesitate herein to do so, but we must learn to try. Vast areas of the peopled world have existed since the beginning of human interaction and most are quite separate from our own in space and time. These various societies have developed independently and from very different roots, experiences, environments, and needs.

Frances Fitzgerald, in his awesome book, *Fire in the Lake*, (the title itself is an ancient Chinese symbol for reversion to what is ancient and true), says that Western culture is the inverse of that of ancient China.[22] We thought the Vietnamese had a small, poor, threatened, old-fashioned culture with a 500 year old economy and technology; and that surely they would welcome us as messianic figures with gratitude and cooperation. What we found, without understanding it at the time, was a proud, ancient culture in crisis.

---

[22] Fitzgerald, Frances. *Fire in the Lake*, Random House, New York, 1972. P. 14

Ancient Chinese Roots

The Vietnamese Culture came out of China long ago (as we shall see from the migration of peoples in the next chapter). That culture developed from pre-historical spiritual forms, which we call Animism and Ancestor Worship, to Taoism, which, as I understand it, is the study of the wisdom of those ancients, and then to the wisdom of Confucius, who made such teachings accessible to the common person by incorporating them into simple sayings. We in the West actually use some of these sayings without crediting their source. Here are a couple of them to remind us:

> "I hear and I forget; I see and I remember; I do and I understand"

> "Before you embark on a journey of revenge, dig two graves."

The good earth was mother to the people and provided not only sustenance but contained the graves of their revered predecessors. It was held in trust for children and grandchildren and harbored for them the continuing spirits of hope and the right way of being. Formal education in the Western style was unknown and would have had little meaning. Where there was education, it was the study of the texts of Confucius, by which notable people were prepared for the Mandarinate. Such scholars then came to represent rightness to the people, as the emperor represented it to them. So were people kept in mind of the traditional ways, by which harmony reigned.

In this system, which idolized the structures of the past, there was no room for things we in the West value, such as creativity, individualism, progress, and the creation of wealth.   Time was not linear and progressive as it is in the West, but rather, circular, moving back to what was true and perfect.

Fitzgerald interviewed the French intellectual, Paul Mus, who lived much of his life in the French Colony of Tonkin (Northern VietNam) and repeats a great story of the passing of a French steamship along the coast of VietNam in the early 19th Century. The local mandarin, instead of rushing to the seashore to investigate this phenomenon, as would a Westerner, went to his study to consult the ancient texts, from which he discovered the object was simply a dragon and would soon pass them by.[23] It did for a while, but then it didn't, and so began the crisis.[24]

I recently asked a student from China, in a school where I sometimes teach, why she chose to come to

---

[23] *Ibid. P. 16*

[24] Note that dragons were important mystical entities to the culture. The many mouths of the MeKong River system are called the "Dragons of the MeKong" because they bring life year after year. The hundreds of limestone islands off the coast in the North of VietNam are traditionally called "Dragon's Teeth". Dragons might be thought of as the spirits of the ancestors, and not therefore dangerous in times of harmony. These mythical creatures morphed into something threatening by the time they got to Medieval Europe.

the U.S. for her education. She responded that in China the teachers only allow a student to read what they direct you to read; and. if a student reads another book, she would be severely disciplined. "We come to America," she said, "to learn how to be creative and think for ourselves." She will be part of the "New" China, which had not yet raised its head in the mid-sixties.

The Village and Tradition

Human association in old China was based on the family, with roles defined as honored father, elder brother, and esteemed uncle; along with its attendant events of birth, life, death, and so on, repeating the same cycle. Values were passed on because they worked in a society that did not evolve very much. If one needed an answer to the problems of life, ask one of the ancients. Life, however, was made possible because of the land. The subsistence crop was and still is rice, and it can be grown in abundance in the warm climate and monsoon rains and by the rivers of S.E. Asia. Rice, by nature however, is a labor-intensive crop and requires a particular social structure and labor force for its cultivation. The village structure developed in support of that crop and that economy. Its pattern was the family, and had the same kind of relationships that held the family together.

A village in VietNam was a system of several hamlets within walking distance of its rice fields. The village was the self-contained system with its special polity, which was derived from the land, the crop, and the revered ancestors. The village not only allowed the people to work together, it sustained them and gave them life. The predominant cultural identity in the land was, therefore, the village and not the family. In times of unrest these villages could become fortified, closed systems and existed quite separate from the rest of the world.

Since distances to any authority were vast and roads nonexistent, few people ever left the areas of their villages and its fields, the village polity and economy was the only known way of life. The social contract was not the aggressive one we share, but rather consisted of the cycle of birth, life, death, and re-birth of the village on land hallowed by the graves of its ancestors. It is not surprising, therefore, that this polity and economy became the pattern for wider rule when such rule became necessary. In the village there were notables who knew rice, notables who cared for people, and so forth, but there was one clear notable who was the father figure; and, as head of the village family, embodied right behavior and harmony to his people. Note the use of the past tense in this discussion. The village has been uprooted and burned along with the society it supported.

Traditional View of Governance and Revolution

Chinese, and then Vietnamese, as a result of these traditions, did not perceive government as the product of a political process. It was simply their way of life under heaven. When the mandarin or the emperor personified harmony in his own being, the heavens were pleased, and the people responded in kind. (There is a leadership lesson here.) When the father figure did not personify such harmony, there was strife in the land, and the father figure no longer held the "Mandate of Heaven."[25] Just as the natural order of time was birth, life, death, rebirth, so was there a cycle of the Mandate of Heaven. As time is circular, so is the mandate; therefore, the nature of revolution is also circular.

We in the West think of revolution as overturning a cultural norm and establishing something entirely new, foreign, and perhaps threatening. To the Sino-Vietnamese culture, revolution is the recovery of harmony and the Mandate of Heaven. It is the return to the strength and vigor of youth.[26] (This finally helped explain for me the Cultural Revolution of Mao ZeDong, in spite of the horrors of that program for the people of China.)

Professor Mus has a story about successful revolution. A mandarin overthrew the emperor in

---

[25] *Fitzgerald.* P. 37
[26] *Ibid.* P. 41.

ancient China and himself became emperor. His first act was to assemble the court musicians and have their instruments smashed, since the previous court was so very obviously out of tune with the Harmony of Heaven. This was not silly superstition, but rather a clear, ritualistic recognition of the return of the court to its legitimate role in reflecting heaven's will.[27]

Buddhism in VietNam

Vietnamese are observers of the virtues of the past, as represented by their predecessors. We call this ancestor worship, but it is much more that that. It is culturally determinative in their concept of circular time. We see they are observers of spirits of the waters, the land, the rice, and other things important to them. We call this animism, but it is far more than that, as they value the life given to them from these things. If you ask a Vietnamese his or her religion, however, most will say, Buddhism, although it normally exists mainly as a figure of the Buddha in the family shrine of ancestors. It is hardly followed as what we would recognize as religion, yet it has a profound societal role.

---

[27] Note that the concept of Heaven is not the same as the Western, specifically Christian understanding. It is more than I can understand, but is the timeless sacred embodiment of right thinking and faithfulness. Harmony is the sign. It is something like our saying, "God is in His Heaven, and all is right with the world."

There are a few pagodas scattered around the cities, and monks and their bonzes follow their rituals. People are glad of it, but do not actively participate – normally. When the Harmony of Heaven is lost in the land, however, the monks emerge like a butterfly from the chrysalis, as a sign to the people that the Will of Heaven has changed and that revolution (as a return to past rightness) is being proclaimed. Fitzgerald says that the Vietnamese people are "Confucians in peacetime, Buddhists in times of trouble."[28] This we will see in the governance of President Diệm, who tried to be a Confucian Father to this society in crisis and failed miserably.

The French had created a feudal society with a near absolute divide between the cities and the villages. In 1963, the Bonzes signaled that the Mandate of Heaven had changed. Revolution was upon the land.

Now, with this introduction to a great cultural disconnect, we turn to the history of the people of VietNam and an account of why and how we ended up in mortal conflict. It is a story we need to remember.

---

[28] Fitzgerald. P. 176.

Part IV: The Approaching Crisis of an Ancient People

There is a lot of history behind the war in VietNam, and all of it is relevant. Here is a very brief summary, although most of this book is by nature history.

The Migration of Peoples to S.E. Asia

Long ago, some peoples came from the islands of Indonesia in small numbers. Their archeological sites have been discovered in the Red River Delta Area and a few sites along the coast further south. Later came some Miao minorities from southern China (Hmong). Ethnic Chinese began moving south into this thinly populated region about 200 BC and formed a loose kingdom in the north, pushing out these older residents, who retreated to the mountains and were later called *Montagnards* (Mountain People) by the French. This was in the area the French later named Tonkin. The name, "VietNam" means "Southern Man, or men who went south – from China. This kingdom was ruled by the Chinese Emperor, who had troops stationed in the area, but in the year 1010, a rebellion occurred and a separate Confucian state was formed which rejected Chinese rule.

Areas further south, later called, Annam and Cochin China by the French (areas we knew as South VietNam), were initially settled by Polynesian sea peoples and peoples moving out of the Indian sub-continent, through what we call Burma and Cambodia. These were known as Khmer and Cham peoples. Khmer areas still exist in the southern delta, and lots to the west of that area, Towers from the Cham period dot the landscape in the highlands to this day. (See my photo of the My Son site in the front of this book.) The name, "Cochin" comes from the word "Khmer".

So, the people of North and South VietNam were initially of different origins, cultures, and even religions. To the North lived the more driven Chinese Buddhist of the Greater Wheel; to the South, the more laid-back Khmer and Cham peoples of the Lesser Wheel.[29] This statement is subject to the understanding of the place of religion in the area; but, it does speak to the more strident, disciplined people in the north, and the more laid-back folk of the south.

The Push South

The Confucian kingdom in the North was confined to the Red River Delta, where rice grew well, but tillable land was quickly occupied. Around the 15th Century, some landless peoples, who had been crowded out, travelled south and created villages growing rice along the coastal areas in the middle of what we know as VietNam. By the 17th Century, they had

---

[29] Although the cultures of both North and South had strong overlays of spirit and ancestor worship, as do many cultures, and with the push south, these traditions began to be similar in various parts of the area.

reached into the rich MeKong Delta of the South. All these areas were inhabited by the above Cham and Khmer peoples and conflict resulted. The various villages became insular, self-sufficient, and "hardened". No help was to come from the north. Distances were great and circumstances of these pioneers were such that connection with the Confucian kingdom of the Red River Delta was broken.

These northern villagers in the South began to push the residents into more remote areas of mountain and delta and even back into Cambodia, from which some of their culture they came.   (This migration and replacement was completed in 1975 with the military conquest of South VietNam.)

In the 17th and 18th centuries the Trinh Lords ruled in the North and the Nguyễn Lords in the South, divided by the natural mountain barrier near the 17th parallel. Then, a Nguyễn named Gia Long succeeded in raising an army in an attempt to conquer the northern Confucian kingdom of Trinh and did so in 1802, making VietNam one political entity (of sorts) for the first time. Having overcome the hated Confucian Kingdom of the north, however, Gia Long then attempted to re-impose the same type government on both north and south to insure his expanded authority. Southerners rebelled, and after 40 years of civil war, the French interceded. The steamship did arrive, after all.

Arrival of the French Colonizers

In the Mid-19th Century, the French were not players in Chinese commerce as were the British and the U.S. They wished access to China, but were frozen out by the other two countries. They had some traders and missionaries in Into-China and knew of the large river system known as the Mekong. They hoped it would lead them by a back-door route into China. Using the pretext that Roman Catholic missionaries were being mistreated, they landed troops and established a naval base at what came to be Saigon. They soon found that the MeKong formed at the Himalayas, and so tried other ways to make their enterprise pay.[30]

They began to build cities in the French Colonial style on old river landing sites (Saigon and Hanoi being the largest examples, though there were many more smaller communities.). They built infrastructure, including the first roads, rails, canals, rubber plantations, and some industry in the north where coal and iron ore were found. When I was in VietNam in 1966 and 67, this infrastructure was evident, though much damaged. It was common to see bridges built by the French destroyed, with a newer bridge beside it, also destroyed, and a U.S. Army bridge beside that one. Saigon was a French city, but with sand bags everywhere and a machine gun emplacement at every intersection, it had lost some of its charm.

---

[30] Fitzgerald. P. 67ff.

I am sure the French thought they were doing a world of good for the Vietnamese people. They even called it the *Mission Civilisatrice*, dispensing the benefits of (French) Civilization to the "primitive" peoples of Asia. Kipling called it the "White Man's Burden" in his 1899 poem of that name, in which he challenges the United States to do right and colonize the Philippines in order to civilize the "New-caught, sullen peoples, half devil and half child."[31]

The whole in vietNam was set up as what I call an extraction colony. Rails were French narrow gauge and led from the rubber plantations to the port and nowhere else. Frederik Logevall wrote extensively of this period in his Pulitzer-winning book, <u>Embers of War</u>. He says that they did little but administer the colonies (in Indo-China) for their own gain.[32] His book title comes from his thesis that we, the Americans, followed in the footsteps of the French, and became prisoners of their experience. "America's intervention occurred," he says in the words of David Halberstam, "in the 'embers' of another colonial war."[33]

---

[31] Rudyard Kipling, "The White Man's Burden: The United States & The Philippine Islands, 1899." *Rudyard Kipling's Verse: Definitive Edition* (Garden City, New York: Doubleday, 1929).

[32] Logevall, Frederik. <u>Embers of War: The Fall of an Empire and the Making of America's VietNam</u>. Random House, New York. 2012. P. 6.

[33] *Ibid*. Preface.

The French administration was focused on Hanoi in the North and Saigon in the South. The large central area was lightly populated, mostly with Montagnards, since it did not lend itself to rice farming as in the South or the eastern fertile and mining areas of the north, so the French divided their conquest into three parts; the North which they called Tonkin, the South, called Cochin China, and the part in the middle they didn't care about called Annam.

People were required to pay tax in money for the first time, so had to go to work for French wages in the mines and on the plantations to gain access to Francs. This began to destroy the village system and the mandarins fled to Hue, which was in Annam (the center), which the French left alone under the pathetic rule of Emperors. At the time of the U.S. entrance to the war, the emperor was Bao Dai, whom the French had found basking on the French Rivera and brought back for the purpose.[34]

Disintegration of the Vietnamese Society

With the erosion of village administration, the French imposed a top-down French rule, which created a new class of civil servants, most of whom lived in the cities. These servants often adopted French ways, religion, and language, further dividing them from the traditionalists who lived in the countryside.[35]   The

---

[34] *Ibid.* P. 75
[35] When my older son and I were in Hanoi in 1999, we found that the oldest people could still speak French. I would tell my son what to say, he would translate it to French, and the

result was a severe feudal society with most people poor and landless and a few wealthy landowners in the cities who depended on private armies to impose their will on the lands and collect rents. The divide between people of the country and of the few cities was to carry over into the U.S. phase of the VietNam War.

The French command could not control the countryside, so attempted to arm proxy fighters to do it for them. Two cults arose, the Cao Dai around Tay Ninh and the Hoa Hao (pronounced "Wah Ho") in the Delta. I have visited the temple of the Cao Dai in Tay Ninh and found a cult of stunning complexity and inclusivity. They propose a synthesis of Roman Catholicism, Secular Humanism, and Confucianism. Their liturgies were elaborate and cathedral-like, and their pantheon of saints include Jesus, Confucius, and Victor Hugo. The French armed both cults to the teeth and created their own fast-strike mobile battalions of Vietnamese soldiers (led by French officers) to project temporary force into the countryside. The unassimilated Cham and Khmer tribes were also armed. There were also some other Catholic groups who formed armies and several war lords in Saigon and the Mekong Delta region thrived on piracy and organized crime including drug trade with approval of the French, provided they were nominally against any resistance to French rule.

---

granddads would translate that to Vietnamese for the others. I wonder what really got through.

This violent mixture naturally began to destroy the village, and people, especially the young, had little choice but to migrate to the cities to join the French administration, the army, or to work in service industries to the French. The economy and society was being slowly disassembled – everything was changing. The deep division that formed between the French and later GVN controlled cities and the countryside was exploited by the VietMinh, and after 1960 by the NLF.

The French response was their mobile strike forces that attempted to respond to enemy activity in the rural areas. The guerillas would strike these road-bound convoys and then melt into the population. The French responded with frustration and indiscriminate force, killing civilians, and increasing hatred toward the occupying force and the Vietnamese who worked for it.[36]

LeLy Hayslip transcribed a song still sung by a mother in the central part of the North as late as the mid-1980s. It follows:

> In our village today
> A big battle was fought,
>> French kill and arrest the People;
>
> The fields and villages burn,
> The People run to the winds;
>> To the North, to the South,
>> To XanHo, to KyLa.

---

[36] Logevall, P. 176.

When they run, they look back;
They see their houses in flames.[37]

Logevall says that when the French resorted to such tactics, Ho Chi Minh had won. Later, when the ARVN mimicked the French, they were beaten; and then the U.S. did the same in the "free fire zones" and massive use of violence, our war was lost as well.

---

[37] Hayslip, LeLy. <u>When Heaven and Earth Changed Places</u>. Doubleday, New York, 1989. P.4.

Part V: World War II
and the Subsequent Politics of Fear

"The Greater East Asian Co-Prosperity Sphere" is a wonderful name created to justify Japanese invasion of China, South-East Asia and Pacific Ocean nations and islands. The intent, of course, was to obtain raw materials and labor for the Japanese homeland. The Imperial Armies had been in China for some years and gained a reputation for brutality there, especially in the 6 weeks of carnage later called the Rape of Nanking.

In a deal with the Axis nations, Vichy France remained in VietNam, and the Japanese were welcomed by them into the three colonies in 1940, taking over most of the administration.[38]

The United States became involved as a result of the Japanese attack on our fleet at Pearl Harbor, which attack was designed to limit our naval response to their taking S.E. Asia. It was a fatal mistake, and the

---

[38] The Japanese used Vietnamese as slave laborers to build military facilities, including carving a small airstrip out of the jungle near Ap Phu Loi, north west of Saigon. From that airstrip, torpedo bombers sortied into the gulf of Thailand and sank two capitol ships of the British Royal Navy. A generation later, I found myself at that airstrip, which had become the forward firebase of the U.S. First Infantry Division.

reason we got involved in fighting the war with Japan in all the Western Pacific, including VietNam.

U.S. Help to the VietMinh in WWII

The VietMinh[39] were a very large and successful resistance movement, which had its roots in opposition to the French in the North. When the French welcomed the Japanese during WWII, the VietMihn carried out guerrilla operations against their new occupier. The United States delivered considerable arms and material support to the VietMinh during that war.

In 1945, a large, celebratory event took place in Hanoi upon the departure of the Japanese. There was a grandstand from which notables addressed the people. U.S. military officers were present.[40]

The celebrated General Võ Nguyên Giáp stated that America was the best friend the Vietnamese ever had. General Giáp was instrumental in fighting the French, the Japanese, the French again, and then the Americans. He was much revered by the people of the North and respected by American Military Leadership.

---

[39] "Việt Minh" is the shortened form of "Việt Nam Độc Lập Đồng Minh Hội," translated as the "League for the Independence of Vietnam". It was formed by Ho Chi Minh at his cave headquarters at Pác Bó, in the North in early 1941.

[40] Baritz. P. 61.

Hồ Chi Minh

Another man, born Nguyễn Sin Cung, quoted from our Declaration of Independence. He was born in 1890 in the large village of Hoang Tru in the North. His father had been a Confucian scholar and mid-level village magistrate for the French, and so Cung was sent to a French school in Hue. This school was also attended by Võ Nguyên Giáp and his later enemy, Ngo Dinh Diệm – a man to was to become President of South VietNam.

Cung began resisting French rule as a student, and was forced to leave. He worked on a French Steamer and saw much of the world. He lived in New York City (Harlem) for several years and even worked for General Motors as a line manager. He drifted to the United Kingdom, working as a waiter and pastry boy. Moving on to France, he became interested in politics, being influenced by his friend, Marcel Cachin, a Socialist Party activist. While there, he became active in the large expatriate Vietnamese community there. Following WWI, he changed his name to Nguyễn Ái Quốc ("Nguyễn the Patriot"), and began to advocate in France for rights for his native VietNam.

Frustrated in this effort, he moved to Moscow in 1923 where he studied at the Communist University of the Toilers of the East before moving on to Canton, China. There he lectured at the Whampoa Military Academy and to young Vietnamese who had fled there to escape the French at home. Contacts made in Canton served him well as he began to plan a return home. He was forced in the interim to move to

Thailand, then India, to Shanghai, and back to the Soviet Union.

In 1938, he returned to China as an advisor to the armed forces. Quốc (formerly "Cung") began regularly using the name "Hồ Chí Minh",[9] a Vietnamese name combining a common Vietnamese surname Hồ, with a given name meaning "He Who has been enlightened", or simply, "Uncle Hồ."[41] Here we see him using traditional roles to gain authenticity in the culture.

In 1940, Hồ returned to VietNam to lead the VietMinh against the French, and the Japanese. He set up headquarters in a cave several hundred miles NW of Hanoi and 100s of people flocked to him; then thousands; then tens of thousands. He formed the VietMinh, which means the "Enlightened People", and attacked French and Japanese patrols and outposts in Tonkin and beyond. By the end of WWII, he had more fighters than the French and Japanese combined.

There were several reasons for this stunning success. First was his nationalist zeal and personal magnetism. Secondly was the hope he brought the people for finally overthrowing the occupiers. Thirdly there was the outside help he received, first from China then the United States. He was supported closely by the U.S. Office of Strategic Services, which furnished a great deal of arms and supplies during

---

[41] "Ho Chi Mihn". from the Wikipedia, the Free Encyclopedia.

WWII. In fact, he was given the code name of "Agent # 19" by the O.S.S. (forerunner of the C.I.A.). Finally, he had developed a carefully-honed and masterful conflation of communist methodology and traditional Vietnamese social structures and mythology. Uncle Hồ was there to stay and a force to be noticed.

Protectorates in the North and South

On 12 August, 1945, the Japanese garrisons in S.E. Asia surrendered. The Allies had a plan for disarming those forces. The Nationalist Chinese took over in Tonkin and British Lord Mountbatten arrived with a small force of Indian troops at Saigon in Cochin China. The Chinese cooperated with the VietMinh to help subdue the Japanese. Of course, later, in 1948, the Nationalists fell back from Mao's forces in China, and that left the VietMinh in complete control. In the South, the British garrison was reinforced by General Douglas Gracey's 20th Indian Division. General Gracey evidently did not speak to the local Vietnamese, but re-armed Japanese troops and their former French prisoners and declared martial law.[42] Vietnamese, understandably, rioted. VietMinh fighters began to move south, and armed encounters ensued. OSS Colonel Peter Dewey reported that if that happened, S.E. Asia would "burn", and he was told to leave Saigon. On his way to the airport, he

---

[42] Prados, John. VietNam: The History of an Unwinnable War, 1945 – 1975. University Press of Kansas, 2009, P. 17 ff.

was ambushed and killed, becoming the first U.S. Casualty of the VietNam War.

So, lets go back to the podium in Hanoi with General Giáp and the great celebration in 1945. The French had gone; the Japanese had gone; a new day had dawned. A squadron of U.S. planes flew over to the cheers of 300,000 Vietnamese as Hồ Chi Minh extolled the virtues of the United States.

Hồ considered the United States to be the great anti-colonial power of the world, and had taken to heart our formational documents, our freeing of the Philippines, and Franklin Roosevelt's vocal support for ending all colonial occupations. President Roosevelt at his meeting with Churchill at Placentia Bay in August of 1941 pushed this policy and insisted it become a part of the Atlantic Charter. He reportedly said, "I can't believe that we can fight a war against fascist slavery and not work to free people all over the world from colonialism." Churchill, ever the colonialist, was in such need of American help, that he did not openly object. The U.S. at the time seemed to hold the high moral ground, and Hồ Chi Minh recognized it.[43]

Hồ had received the cold shoulder from the Soviet Union, which was intent on taking over Eastern Europe. He didn't trust the Chinese, and once said that the last time the came to VietNam they stayed 1000 years.

---

[43] Logevall, P. 48f.

Over the next six months, Hồ Chi Minh sent eight letters to President Truman trying to forge an alliance with the U.S. to help build a new nation. None of his letters were answered.[44] The reason was that a large problem loomed. He was, after all, a Communist of sorts, and therefore everything had changed.

In March of 1999, my son, John, and I were traveling in the North of VietNam with a party-member guide. On the way from Hanoi to HaLong Bay, she asked me why Americans tried to colonize the South? I replied that we had no such intent. "We were a colony, ourselves, not that long ago," I said, "and we didn't much like it." "Then, why did you come?" she reasonably asked. I replied that it was because Nikita Khrushchev pounded his shoe on the table and promised to "Bury us all," and we believed him. (She also spoke of Joseph Stalin as "Father Stalin.") I who thought of the U.S. as acting from high moral ground in the war, was reminded that the rest of the world does not see us the same way.

The Rising Soviet Threat and the Cold War

Following WWII, the Soviets occupied Eastern Europe with a vengeance and set about broadcasting their totalitarian ideology. It would have been very unpopular for any U.S. President to support even a nominally-communist leader. President Roosevelt died in office on 17 April 1944, and his successor showed little knowledge of his ideas for S.E. Asia and

---

[44] Baritz. P. 61.

was quite concerned with building up France to offset the increasing imperial sounds and threats coming from Moscow.   Everything had changed.

President Truman established what came to be known as the "Truman Doctrine," which was a pledge to use the power of the U.S. to resist Communist expansion anywhere in the world.[45]   This expansionism was not a misinterpretation of the facts. It was clearly the policy of the Soviet Union, expressed in so many words by Joseph Stalin, himself. He saw Moscow as the center for pan-global Communist rule.[46]

There was, therefore, good reason for the Truman Doctrine, but this commitment forced us to recognize France as the colonial power in VietNam, making Hồ Chi Minh our enemy.   France's General deGaul, who sat out the war in London, played the communist card, saying that unless the U.S. helped France regain her former power and influence, they could not stem the tide of communism in France and Europe. He defined this not only as building up French forces at home, but also the recovery of French Colonies in South-East Asia.   Truman did not respond to Hồ, but did to deGaul, providing arms and ships to transport French troops back to their former colonies, (eventually to include the French Foreign Legion, by then made up mainly of former SS troopers.)[47]   Within

[45] McCullough, David. Truman. Simon & Schuster, New York, 1992. P. 582.
[46] Caplow, Theodore and Hicks, Louis. Systems of War and Peace University Press of American, New York, 2002. P. 188.

months, there were 65,000 French Troops in VietNam, paid for in large part by the United States, in a stunning reversal of the anti-colonialist policy of President Roosevelt.

The Soviets got the atomic bomb in 1948, and we children practiced "Duck and Cover" in our classrooms. Everything changed for children as well. President Eisenhower in his address to the United Nations in 1952 said that there is a new language, the language of Atomic Warfare.[48]

Near the end of WWII, The Soviet Union belatedly invaded Manchuria in a deal with the United States to put pressure on the Japanese from the north-west. They went in hard with a million men and enough of our Lend-Lease hardware to crush Japan's famed Kwantung Army. Richard Bernstein reports in his new book that this included 2700 artillery pieces, 5500 tanks, and 3700s planes. When the Soviet Army departed, they turned over to Mao Zedong all the captured Japanese military hardware and much of the equipment we supplied.[49] This gave Mao ascendancy over his rival, and in October of 1949, Chiang Kai-Shek fled Mainland China, and the Communist system under Mao ZeDong took over. A

---

[47] Prados. P. 19.
[48] Prosser, Michael H. Sow the Wind, Reap the Whirlwind, Volume I, William Morrow & Co., New York. 1970, P. 75.
[49] Bernstein, Richard. China 1945: Mao's Revolution and America's Faithful Choice. Knopf Publishing, 2014, as reported by the Author in the Washington Post, Book Review Section, 12 Dec 2014.

good part of this defeat, of course, was due to the hated class system of the Nationalists and the genius of Mao. The Nationalists fled to Formosa (Taiwan), and into the "Golden Triangle" where they existed, partly by developing the Opium crop, until found there by the CIA, armed, and used against Lao insurgents and infiltrating VietMinh and NVA during the VietNam War.

Losing China was a huge shock to the West, and a political bombshell in this country. No one in any political party could have avoided this loss, but everyone wanted to avoid the blame. The anti-communist attitude, platforms, and slogans in all Political Parties in the U.S. hardened as a result. No politician wanted to be seen as, "Soft on Communism." Once again, our short-sightedness helped create the culture which made the VietNam War, in Baritz's word, "Inevitable."

By 1954, both the French and the VietMinh had large numbers of soldiers and war-making capability in Tonkin. It is estimated that Hồ, equipped with U.S. Weapons from Korea and some left by the Japanese, had 100,000 regular troops, 50,000 regional troops, and 255,000 part-time guerrillas, far more than the French. Both sides used the rich opium poppy fields in the north-west to finance their war. The French, seeking to draw the VietMinh into a set-piece battle, set up a garrison, 13,000 strong, at Dien Bien Phu – right in the middle of that rich poppy farming area which furnished much-needed cash for both sides. There was also a geo-political reason for this location. The VietMinh had moved into Laos and their army was threatening to overrun Vientiane, and this position in the west of the country was a good place to mount mobile interdictions of VietMihn movements and supply lines. The French were daring Hồ to do something about it. He did. What he did became a pattern they would try to repeat in 1968 at Khe Sanh.

Hồ patiently built concealed roads for hundreds of miles to support his plan and moved forces to block any avenues of escape or reinforcement and attacked. The garrison eventually fell, and the remaining French soldiers were marched on foot 500 miles. Only 3000 survived, and the French army collapsed. The U.S. moved into Cochin China in the south to block the VietMinh from taking Saigon, and the stage was set in an attempt to make the people of the South our blocking force for what many in American thought was a concerted drive of Communism into areas traditionally controlled by the West.[50]

In addition, Cochin China was the breadbasket of S.E. Asia, and the people of Tonkin and Annam depended upon it for the staple food supply, so the lack of access to crops from the South was unacceptable to the land-poor North.

Our Allies of World War II in the southern Pacific, Australia and New Zealand, seemed threatened. Thailand, Cambodia, Malaya, Burma, and especially Laos seemed sure to fall like dominos (a phrase coined by President Eisenhower).

---

[50] Baritz. P. 87.

In Signal Mountain, Tennessee, my friends and I joined the Ground Observer Corps and rode our bicycles to weekly tours scanning the skies from the bell tower of a monastery, looking for Russian bombers. We were to report immediately any aircraft that flew within sight, but we never saw planes of any kind. That is a good thing, since they didn't furnish us with a telephone. We didn't know at the time that no Russian plane had the range to reach into the interior of the United States.

In February of 1950, Senator Joseph McCarthy gave a speech to the Ohio County Women's Republican Club in Wheeling, West Virginia, claiming to have a list of hundreds (the number kept changing) of State Department employees who were members of the Communist Party and who were influencing Foreign Policy.[51] He hammered this theme home, waving a "list" and built it into a political base, though no list was ever submitted to the government, although the F.B.I. was actively looking for infiltration by that time.[52]

There was much acceptance of these allegations in the wake of activities of Alger Hiss and like Soviet operatives and sympathizers as well as the theft of the secrets that gave the Soviets our nuclear weapons technology. McCarthy's subsequent "Army-McCarthy" hearings were very popular witch-hunts in a country near war-fever over suspected, and often

---

[51] Griffith, Robert, Joseph R. McCarthy and the Senate. University of Massachusetts Press, 1970. p. 49

[52] Joseph McCarthy was successful only in stirring up the country, and died at age 49 of alcoholism. (Wikipedia)

real, Communist infiltration. There would be no "Fifth Column", as in Norway; no appeasement such as Neville Chamberlain wrought at Munich – each a lesson from WWII.

The National Security Council advised the President Truman that the South and South East Asian areas would be swept by Communism, producing a "Major political rout." This seemed to be the case as four wars raged in the sub-continent. Logevall says that "Apocalyptic Anti-Communism" prevailed and most Americans believed that all Asian peoples and nations were alike and all were threatened by a monolithic Communism controlled by Moscow. This was reinforced when both Russia and China after WWII rushed to recognize the new government of Hồ Chi Minh in the North. The United States immediately recognized the government of Bao Dai. The U.S. allies followed in 1950 and 1951.

Meanwhile, popular opinion in France had turned against the war. Pierre Mendes France, of the (not so) Radical Party proclaimed, "As long as we go on loosing all these officers and men in Indo-China; as long as we go on spending 500 billion francs a year, we shall have no army in Europe, and only 500 billion francs worth of inflation, poverty, and fuel for Communist propaganda."[53] All of Europe stood against our intervening and asked us to open negotiations with the VietMinh, but our Administrations and our public would have none of it. NSC-124, approved by President Truman, stated that

---

[53] Logevall, P. 313.

if France withdrew from Indo-China, we would engage the war ourselves, and that if China intervened, we would attack China.[54]

Then came the attack of North Korea against the South. Again, we felt that we had proof of the Communist threat. In fact, famed French General Jean deLattre deTassigny, creator of the *Groupes Mobiles* force in VietNam, toured the United States proclaiming that the war in Indo China and the war in Korea were part of the same conflict.[55]

Some of you might have fought in Korea. Thank you for your service in what was the first proxy war between the U.S.S.R. and the United States. Neither the Soviet Union nor the United States wanted to confront the other directly because of the potential for nuclear war; so, we did it through third nations, such as North and South Korea and North and South VietNam. In fact, to many in the U.S, Korea and VietNam were part of the same challenge. If we intervened in one, why not the other?

In each case, China became involved - with ground troops in the case of Korea. This was one of the great fears regarding VietNam - that China would join the war. They didn't, but the mortars and rockets that fell on us in PhuLoi and the enemy's Kalashnikov

---

[54] NSC-124/2, June 25, 1952. "United States – VietNam Relations, 1945 – 1967", Study Prepared by the Department of Defense. Government Printing Office, Washington, D.C, 1971, 8:531-534.
[55] Logevall, P. 283.

rifles were made in China. Interestingly, much later in an interview with Henry Kissinger, Mao ZeDong said that he had made three major mistakes in his lifetime. One was intervening in the Korean War. The second was the Cultural Revolution. The third was supporting the North in the VietNam War.[56] I don't know for sure if Mao was sincere in his reported regret, but can attest to some of the cost of these decisions.

Caplow and Hicks, sociologists of warfare at the University of Virginia and St. Mary's College of Maryland, respectively, report that there were 80 proxy wars during the "Cold War" period and that these wars caused 30 million deaths. The "Cold War" was hot for a lot of nations and people.[57]

The Soviets developed heavy-lift rockets and put Sputnik in orbit. I remember listening to its beep. Then Yuri Gagarin orbited in April of 1961, to our embarrassment and fear. We high school students flocked to the sciences, eschewing any perspective the disciplines of history, languages, geography, political science, or art might have given us.

That same month brought the Bay of Pigs debacle, after which neither President Kennedy nor President Johnson trusted or listened seriously to either the CIA

---

[56] Kissinger, Henry. On China, Penguin Books, New York, 2012.

[57] Caplow and Hicks. P. 64.

or the Military Chiefs. Then came the Cuban Missile Crisis, and the confrontation became real and immediate. President Kennedy was urged to move the government from D.C, but refused. What made the Cuban crisis so very dangerous was that the proxy methodology got out of hand and we were in a direct confrontational mode. The country, indeed the world, felt on the brink of Armageddon.

Up went the Berlin Wall in 1961, along with the level of anti-West rhetoric from Moscow. President Kennedy met with Khrushchev in Vienna, and was badly beaten up by him publicly. Kennedy came home thinking VietNam was a good place to counter-punch and sent Vice-President Johnson to Saigon. Johnson returned saying that President Diệm was, "The Winston Churchill of Asia."

Competitive, atmospheric nuclear testing warned of the end of habitable earth.[58] The Soviets sent tanks into Hungary and we had more evidence of their wish to dominate the world. It was a most unsettling time.

This context of near-hysteria is key to understanding our going to war in Vietnam. It prevailed for the entire decade following. In November of 1961, the 57th and 8th Transportation Helicopter Companies deployed aboard U.S.N.S. Core to VietNam along with associated field maintenance, medical, and signal

---

[58] Kennedy, John F. Address to the United Nations of 25 September 1961: "Every inhabitant of this planet must contemplate the day when this planet might no longer be habitable."

detachments.[59] Their mission was to carry supplies to ARVN units in the field, but they soon were carrying the Republics soldiers as well. So did everything change for us, for VietNam, and for the world.

Now that the stage for intervention by the United States is set, I want to take a break from this history to fill out one more aspect of the coming conflict – how it would be fought. This, too, is a cultural issue.

---

[59] Knight, Emmett F. <u>First In VietNam: An Exercise in Excess of 30 Days,</u> Authorhouse, 2014. P. 7.

Part VI: Culture determines a Nation's way of making war

(and sometimes insuring defeat.)

Different cultures go to war for different reasons and fight in different ways. Caplow and Hicks say that the way a nation fights is dependent on the status pattern and the technological levels of the surrounding society.[60]

Our Particular Way of Making War

Part of our National Mythology is that we are a people who have huge resources and technologically-advanced weaponry. We can bring formidable management skills to the production and utilization of these weapons and live in relative comfort at the same time. We can win on a conventional battlefield with this kind of fighting force. We proved it in WWII, but since, because of the nuclear capability of both camps, things changed.

The Soviet Union chose to use their subjugated satellite countries to push the boundaries and limits of their ambition, and these weaker countries engaged in wars of insurgency with their neighbors, even in our hemisphere. And so began those "Proxy Wars." This was a major challenge for U.S. Administrations..

---

[60] Caplow and Hicks. P. 75.

Guerrilla warfare, is foreign to us. We could not defeat an enemy in VietNam whom we couldn't recognize, and which would usually choose not to stand and fight. We could not counter their Strategy of Revolutionary War with firepower alone, though we tried.

The ancient infantry maxim of, "Find them; Fix them; Fight them; Finish them," did not apply. We couldn't do any of the four when the enemy simply melted into the population or back into Cambodia or Laos at will.

President Kennedy looked at the Viet Cong Guerrilla and admired his toughness and leanness and, against the advice of the Pentagon, formed the Special Forces. According to Loren Baritz, President Kennedy reasoned that if a Viet Cong soldier could lie under water and breath through a straw, an American with the proper training and a really nice straw could do it better. [61]

Baritz suggests that breathing through a straw will not win a guerrilla war - getting out of the water and mingling with the local population without being noticed might. Giant, non-Asian Americans could never do that in Vietnam. I don't think Baritz quite understands the VietNam Era mission of the Special Forces as trainers of paramilitary fighters, but the characterization is instructive.

Our leadership did not adapt to this change in the way of making war, so we fought in the only way we knew.

---

[61] Baritz. P. 322.

Until General Abrams took over from General Westmoreland, the bulk of the U.S. Army hunkered down at night in base camps all over the South and during the day engaged in large-unit sweeps .[62]

Large Scale Operations and Heavy Weapons

Cedar Falls was one of the large operations in which I was involved in 1967.[63] We used classic European-theater tactics with artillery, blocking forces, armor, airborne units, and air power. This is the way we were taught to fight, and the Army did not want to change its training, because the dominant thinking remained that our major threat was the invasion of Western Europe by the U.S.S.R. Cedar Falls was carried out by Big Red One, the First Infantry Division and Tropic Lighting, the 25th Infantry Division, reinforced with an airborne battalion. The Army of South VietNam, the ARVN, was (as usual until much later) nowhere to be seen.

Such operations, each involving as many as 30,000 G.I.s, destroyed the peoples' livelihoods and

---

[62] Although, as the war went on, the Army learned and adapted. The use of airmobile units is one example. Another, writes General Palmer (The 25 Year War, page 156) is that our heavy infantry was lightened up so that they could move more quickly through the countryside.
[63] Another of these major Search and Destroy operations when I was there was Operation Junction City in March of '67, which included the largest airborne operation since Operation Market Garden during World War II.

ancestral villages without catching many enemy combatants, and they turned the people against us and against their government. The Southerners among us still remember Sherman's march through Georgia, do we not.

These sweeps were, however, very effective in driving the NLF and NVA to the edges of the country and beyond, for a time. Whether or not this is a good idea depends on what kind of war you are fighting.

Such operations point out the failings of the "Base Camp" idea, by which large numbers of Army personnel were drawn into fortified camps from which they could foray into the countryside and kill the enemy (as in the major operation described above). This division of soldier and population, base camp and the fields of battle, had the psychological effect of making all Vietnamese seem to be enemies and exposed the population to the VC and NVA cadres whenever we were not in the field. General Palmer calls it our most pernicious policy, in that it, "Soaked up huge amounts of personnel and waste of material resources, and required us to defend and take care of these albatrosses (the base camps)."[64]

We used what weapons we had and knew, such as B-52 bombers that carpet-bombed jungle with little target identification.

We utilized huge amounts of artillery. I remember our being hit on the night of 29 July 67 by the 3rd North

[64] Palmer. P. 69.

Vietnamese Rocket Artillery Battalion, reinforced with mortar and 12.7 mm antiaircraft batteries. 49 one-twenty-two mm rockets and 89 rounds of mortar fire landed on Firebase PhuLoi. We responded with 2744 rounds of artillery plus mortars, and the next morning found one KIA and one blood trail. We had three KIA, 31 WIA, and lots of helicopters damaged or destroyed.[65] Here is a fact for you: We expended more explosive power in that war than was expended by all sides in WWII – 7.6 million tons of bombs alone.

Westmoreland, an old Artillery Officer, was asked in a press conference how to fight insurgents. His unfortunate answer was "Firepower". We dropped 70 tons of bombs per square mile on that country according to General Thayer's book.[66]

That is the equivalent of 51,000 tons of high explosives dropped on Albemarle County in Virginia over a ten year period; plus our massive use of artillery, which in the South averaged 1 million rounds per month for the year I was in-country. That is in excess of the combined equivalent of both nuclear weapons dropped on Japan at the end of WWII - in Albemarle County alone! Bear in mind as you process those numbers that both North and South Vietnam would fit inside California, with room to spare

---

[65] U.S. MACV, VietNam, "PAVN Artillery (Rocket Units) Intelligence Study", Indochina Archive, University of California, 1967, P. A-7
[66] Thomas Ricks, quoting General Thayer's, War Without Fronts: The American Experience in VietNam , Westview Special Studies in Military Affairs, 1985. Out of Print.

Strategy of the North

So, was this level of violence necessary? The best answer I have is no, and yes. I have read several books on this question, some of them by hawks and some not. What is clear is that the North had determined designs on the South and made careful plans by 1960 to take it by what they called the Strategy of Revolutionary War. Phillip Davidson writes about this very clearly and shows the intent of the North in that they kept cadre in the south all along and actually moved the 325th Infantry Division into the highlands of VietNam in 1964. The insurrection in the South was by then supported by the North, and when possible, main force NLF and NVA soldiers were used against suitable targets.

Davidson says this strategy integrates armed conflict and political conflict (*Dau Tranh*) leading to seizure of national power. The military part of this plan had three phases:[67] These military phases are:

a. When the state is stronger, fight as guerrillas
b. When there is a parity of forces, combine guerrilla and conventional warfare.
c. When there is strength, use total, conventional warfare to defeat the enemy.

If the counter-strategy of the U.S. Military had been to match these phases, it would then have used very

---

[67] Davidson, Phillip B. (Lt. Gen Rtd.) Secrets of the VietNam War. Prisidio Press, CA. 1990. P. 18.

different responses to phase "a", and phase "b". Furthermore, there might be different phases extant in the country at the same time, and the phases could shift back and forth according to relative strength. This means that at some times and at some places, huge application of power is required, such as in response to the invasion of the North into *Quang Tri* Provence after withdrawal of U.S. ground troops. Likewise, during times and places of insurgency, use of force on the scale of war in Europe is not going to win over the people.

An integral part of the plan of the North to defeat the South was Political *Dau Tranh* (struggle). This component included political and sociological teaching to its personnel and the people of the South. It was intended to mobilize the people in support of the NLF fighters, indoctrinate the people against the GVN, and win over ARVN soldiers to the cause. It is clear, therefore, that the whole plan begins with Insurgency.[68]

The Nature of Insurgency

An Chaired professor of political science at Williams College named James McAllister, in "Who Lost Vietnam?" writes that Westmoreland knew our military couldn't do counterinsurgency and thought we could leave it to the South Vietnamese Army.[69] The fact is,

---

[68] *Ibid.* P. 19.
[69] James McAllister. "Who Lost VietNam:" Soldiers, Civilians, and U.S. Military Strategy", <u>International Security Journal</u>, v

though, that we had built and equipped that army in our conventional image to fight in our way, as if their enemy was to be the Soviets at Fulda Gap.

The Vietnamese Government, around 1963, built five light infantry divisions to occupy the countryside, but General Harkins (who preceded Westmoreland) told them they were wasting the assets we had given them. They were re-formed as heavy divisions, which were largely useless in the countryside where the war was being lost.[70] Interestingly enough, the response of the Ninth Plenum of the Party Central Committee in the North was to improve the Hồ Chi Minh Trail through Laos to accommodate trucks. Increased pressure by the U.S led to regular NVA soldiers moving into the South in force, beginning with the 325th Division.[71]

All this was the wrong strategy, writes General Bruce Palmer in his incredible study titled, The 25 Year War. He shows that throughout the war, we violated as a matter of policy all six accepted Classical Principals of War, which each officer memorized as part of his education.[72] I remember them still: Objective, Offensive, Mass, Maneuver, Economy of Force, and Unity of Command. We will revisit these in a moment and discuss how they might better have applied.

35, Issue 3, P.95ff.

[70] Ricks. P. 225.

[71] Prados. P. 114.

[72] Bruce Palmer, Jr. The 25-Year War: America's Military Role in VietNam. Simon & Schuster, Inc, New York, 1984.

Palmer argues that if good communication and trust existed between the President and the Military Chiefs, a strategy that met these principles could have been successful without the level of violence we used.

As it as, we looked at the people's villages and considered them primitive, though they served very well, were the source of their economy and their society, and contained in their soil the sacred graves of their ancestors. In an attempt to deny the enemy the support of the villagers, we moved hundreds of thousands into enclosed, "strategic hamlets" we built for them. This number later rose to as much as half of the nation's population, which crowded into shacks built of refuse in huge ghettos around the cities.

That made it possible to burn their villages and create free-fire zones. John Paul Vann said that "' Zippo jobs' on Vietnamese hamlets by American soldiers became so common that television audiences in the United States were no longer scandalized by them."[73] The fortified hamlets we built became important recruiting centers for the Viet Cong. This resettlement also destroyed the food supply of the country, so we sent ships of rice from Texas.

[73] Neil Sheehan. A Bright Shining Lie: John Paul Vann and America in VietNam, Random House, New Yorkm 1988, P. 589.

Counter-Productive Nature of Extreme Violence

Pretty much everything we did for the first half of the war taught the South Vietnamese people to hate us and their own government (GVN), and schooled their government and their army to sit back and do nothing.

The roads and rivers were dangerous to G.Is, so we used Agents Orange, White, Blue, and Purple to defoliate the jungle and destroy crops.

Many GIs were saved by this practice, perhaps myself included. Today, there is comparatively little jungle left, but lots of herbicide-related illness and deformity in subsequent generations of children. This I have seen first-hand, especially in the Delta.

To give credit where it is due, the Marines in I Corps did far better at counter-insurgency than did the Army. In fact, Westmoreland reviled the Marines for going easy on the enemy. This is not quite so cut and dried as it might seem. Remember General Davidson and the third phase of the North's Strategy of Revolutionary War. That phase is total war. For the Marines on the DMZ or at Khe Sanh the war was always conventional, total warfare. For them, Westmoreland's concern was appropriate. For the Marines in the DaNang area and further south in I Corps, however, the CAP program and counter-insurgency made more sense.[74]

---

[74] Davidson. P. 25.

Another reason for Westmoreland's attitude was that the Army seemed to re-invent guerrilla warfare every time, whereas the Marine Corps wrote a manual for fighting insurgents, drawing on their experience in the Philippines in the Spanish-American War. It was published in 1940, and with its update of 2002 is still used. It is called, "The Small Wars Manual".[75] (To be fair, the Army now has one as well.)

James Joes, in his book, America and Guerrilla Warfare, describes the background for the Marine manual and notes that the way we fought then established the basis for an enduring friendship between Americans and Filipinos:

> *"There were no screaming jets accidentally bombing helpless villages, no B-52s, no napalm, no artillery barrages, no collateral damage.*
>
> *Instead, the Americans conducted a very decentralized war of small mobile units armed mainly with rifles in conjunction with native Filipinos.*

They were very successful, as were the British using the same tactics in Malaya; so, the extreme violence of VietNam during the insurgency phase, places, and

---

[75] United States Marine Corps. Small Wars Manual, Department of the Navy, 1940. Also see: "Small Wars", Addendum to the Manual, 2004.

times was not only unnecessary, it was counter-productive.

Would the peasants in the countryside adopt our way of life and polity in spite of this level of violence, even though there was no tradition for it in their culture? Not likely, I think.

So, to summarize thus far: our cultural mythology determined our going to war, and it determined our means of war; but, in the insurgency phases of this war, the means destroyed the supposed purpose, and we were stuck in the proverbial "Catch 22".

We performed well in military engagements, and fought in the only way we knew how to fight in an unknown cultural sea, but we fought without the likelihood of meeting any cultural objectives of the South Vietnamese people.

Things had changed, and the war kept changing, but our strategy and tactics did not keep up. We did not understand the strategy of the enemy and had little of our own. This was a huge failure of vision and leadership, both Political and Military.

Part VII: Successes and Failures of Leadership on Both Sides of the Pacific

When the French were defeated in Tonkin after having lost Dien Bien Phu, we took over responsibility for Cochin China in the South and created and signed the Southeast Asia Collective Defense Treaty in 1955, intended to prevent Communism from spreading. The principle statesmen involved were Harry Truman and John Foster Dulles. There were nine signatory countries, although Wikipedia tells me that the only real participants in S.E. Asia were the Philippines and Thailand, but I remember Korean (ROK) Marines near us who were a force that didn't mess around. VietNam was not considered a nation, but a protectorate, so was not a signatory. Nevertheless, that country was the true focus of the next perceived step in the onward march south of Communism.

Meanwhile, that little fledgling country was flying apart from within. By 1959 the North had begun opening a trail through Laos and Cambodia to the south. The VietMinh morphed in the South to become the NLF (National Liberation Front) in 1960. By 1962, it is estimated that 80% of villages in the South were involved with the NLF, and Fitzgerald writes that a Marxist/Leninist party had gained ascension and had begun to plan and establish the political indoctrination wing of the front.[76] In two more years the number of

85

villages had increased to a reported 90%, including the suburbs of Saigon.

I remember in 1967 watching the interrogation of a suspected (probable) NLF soldier by ARVN personnel. It was not a pretty thing to see. Not that NLF soldiers didn't use methods that were cruel and repugnant, but there was a political difference. The government of South Vietnam (GVN) existed in force and not in the peoples' hearts. When GVN troops (Army of VietNam - ARVN) entered a village, they arrived in uniforms that looked like those of the hated French. They treated them with arrogance and used their power to coerce, steal and subjugate. Then, as dark threatened, they left.

The NLF and Leadership

The VietMinh had a story that was created by Uncle Hồ in the early 1940s, in accordance with his Strategy of Revolutionary War, previously mentioned. By the time of the war in Korea, he had begun making contacts in the South, and by 1960, the NLF cadres were taught this message (more in a moment). They arrived in the villages teaching in effect that their revolution offered a way back into the old ways of their ancestors – back to the Harmony of Heaven.[77] They reminded the people that their soldiers came from the villages themselves and not from the hated French. They taught three duties and five virtues.

---

[76] Fitzgerald. P.192.
[77] *Ibid.* P. 193

The duties were to prince, father, and husband – a system somewhat familiar to the villagers. The five virtues were: benevolence, righteousness, propriety, knowledge, and sincerity.

Furthermore, the NLF had a program of indoctrination for all its recruits. There were twelve points of discipline, eight of which governed the soldiers' conduct toward the villagers and people of the countryside, (but not GVN or ARVN personnel or most city dwellers.) These points show clearly that they had a sophisticated understanding of what worked in their culture and what did not. These eight points were:

- Be Fair
- Be Polite
- Take Nothing
- Damage Nothing
- Live and Eat with the People
- Dress as do the People
- Love the People
- Ask the People for Help

It was a long way from the attitude of the bullying soldiers of the GVN. It is also a long way from the flame throwers and bombs of U.S. forces. Violence is not the way to win a war of insurgency.

Note however, that the above list of behaviors was the persona the NLF adopted in order to gain the trust of people in the South, especially in the countryside. The NLF could be quite stunningly cruel and often were. For instance, read the Prologue to Tom Campbell's wonderful book, The Old Man's Trail, which has an account of the horrors perpetrated by the 267th Battalion during the 1968 Tet Offensive in Saigon. It is full of murder of children, burning with gasoline of whole families, shooting of Buddhist Monks, and cutting off heads of American Officers with det cord, forcing a little girl to push the igniter. The scale of horror was even worse in Hue.[78]

The culture of the South did not prepare villagers to be good soldiers or administrators. Earlier we spoke of the Village system being based on relationships that could be described as those of honored father, elder brother, and esteemed uncle, regardless of whether or not these people were blood relatives. The terms describe intimate authority and filial relationships which do not come easily, but from generations of rice farming.

Remember also that the villages had always been closed systems and isolated from the world. Most young men had never been further away from home than the next village. This made it difficult for them to adapt to a military life in which these relationships had to be left behind.

The soldiers and administrators in the GVN, were placed in a Western hierarchical system in which they felt no loyalty or trust, only mutual suspicion, so they sat and pretty much did nothing other than work the

---

[78] Campbell, Tom. The Old Man's Trail. Naval Institute Press, Annapolis. 1995. Prologue.

system for whatever benefit it might give them and plot to protect their status from everyone else. The U.S. command discovered that in the twelve years of war leading up to 1966, only one ARVN field grade officer had been wounded and none killed in fighting.[79] Fitzgerald talks about this as well, saying that distrust was paralyzing throughout the system.

The NLF, however, insisted on organized "reeducation", and treated the recruit like the younger brother for an extended period of time until each person could take a productive place in the system and become an elder brother to someone else.

It is time to talk about Hồ Chi Minh again. While in Paris, he became acquainted with the writings of Marx and Lenin, and saw in it a parallel to the culture of his native people. The revolution of marginalized workers of Europe sounded much like the oppressed village farmers of his own country. Breaking the grip of the capitalist class sound a lot like throwing off the yoke of the imperialist French. He found that he could cast the communist message in ways that were not Stalinist, but more pure in form and similar to the Confucian style of being together in harmony. When he arrived in the North from China in 1940, he set about teaching these things to the VietMinh to give them a political culture that brought unity to the fighters and supporters against the invader who was about a different type of revolution.

---

[79] *Ibid.* sP. 427, 270ff.

One part of this teaching sounds very suspect to a Westerner, that is the required "self criticism" sessions. (Hồ was, after all, a Communist.) These sessions were not concerned with learning about the self, however, but rather about re-forming the group into a family system. Hồ called it *KhiemThao*. Fitzgerald credits this practice with creating a new culture among the VietMinh, and later the NLF, in which each level of the fighting force trusted one another and their superiors and subordinates. A commander could report truth to his superior even when it was bad news. This did not happen in ARVN, where commanders would cover up bad news so it would not reflect negatively on them. It is said that around 30% of ARVN soldiers were missing at any one time and not reported as such. This meant that the generals never knew the strength of their formations and that the commanders were collecting and pocketing the pay for the missing men.[80]

The soldiers of the NLF were very effective, working out of hidden areas and using the villages as supply depots and even barracks. Often there were underground storehouses, quarters, and hospitals just outside villages. The village took care of the soldiers, and they cared for the villagers.[81] All this was the direct result of the leadership of Hồ and the failure of the GVN to be friends to the people. Rather, the government in Saigon became more and more corrupt and remote. The fragmentation continued. South VietNam approached complete collapse.

---

[80] *Ibid.* P. 276
[81] *Ibid.* P. 216.

Total Conventional War

We have seen that extreme violence is counter-productive in a war of insurgency. This is not the case when war reaches other phases. For instance, Hồ's Strategy of Revolutionary War, third phase, is total warfare. It is Grant charging after Lee's Army of Northern Virginia in the Overland Campaign. It is the Russian assault on Berlin. It is a no-holds barred conflict. We shall see in a later chapter, that President Johnson never quite got it that these are two different wars. He used too much force for the first and tied the hands of Westmoreland for the second. Since the enemy was calling the shots, the North maintained the initiative most of the time. Since our leadership didn't seem to understand this, we did not hold the initiative, most of the time.

When the U.S. withdrew ground forces, the equation of relative power was altered, and the North went to the third phase of their plan. They invaded with overwhelming force, and won the war over an already fragmented, defeated South. Lets look for a moment at why it was a defeated country by that time.

President Ngo Dinh Diệm

To lead the country of South VietNam, we supported the wrong leader in a make-shift government. His name was Ngô Đình Diệm. He was a mid-level mandarin from Hue in Annam who had fled to the United States, where he made enough noise to attract the attention of the Administration. He then went on to Paris, where he worked the large, influential expatriate Vietnamese community. These people lobbied Emperor Bao Dai to appoint him Prime Minister, which he did. We supported the choice because he was most like us; and, as a consequence, most unlike the people he was supposed to govern.

Diệm was a French-Educated, Catholic, Mandarin from Hue in a country where most people hated all four. When he arrived in Saigon to take over the government as Prime Minister, appointed by Bao Dai, he had everything stacked against him. The South was, as we have seen, deeply divided between a few cities and everywhere else. Support in the villages was nil. Everywhere, the government was challenged by major armed groups.

There was the VietMinh, later the NLF and their troops in the countryside.[82] The Hoa Hao in the MeKong Delta and Cao Dai in the West had thousands of trained men under arms. The Bay Vien was a bandit organization controlling half of SaiGon. The Binh Zuyen followers were a huge, armed, crime family. The Cochin Chinese Landlords still extracted rents from the villages through armed gangs or South

---

[82] The NLF was the National Liberation Front, which came into being in 1960 to organize groups and villages in the countryside. Their soldiers turned out to be excellent light infantry and were known by the U.S. and GVN as VC, or VietCong, which itself was short for ViệtNam CộngSảm, or Communist Man.

Vietnamese soldiers on the pad. The Buddhists were usually not armed, but some sects were. There were anti-Catholic traditionalists, anti-mandarin, anti-Hue groups, likewise armed. There were the French, and there were ARVN officers themselves with divided loyalties.[83]

Diệm had absolutely no power base other than in Washington. One expedient was to relocate loyal people from the North. The U.S. 7th Fleet in Operation "Passage to Freedom" transported 860,000 Roman Catholics from the North during the migration protocol established by the Geneva Accords of 1954. This migration gave him some kind of constituency in the South.[84] That, of course, immediately angered most Southerners, few of whom were either northerners or Roman Catholics. Diệm set himself up as a Confucian Mandarin and ignored the structures that existed in the government. He appointed a cabinet of his own family and actually conspired against his own government to make sure his will was not thwarted.

Prime Minister Diệm promptly disavowed the Geneva Accords, especially the elections called for within two years. (Remember that no officials from VietNam, north or south, were invited to Geneva; the countries had no standing and were not signatories.)[85] Had the elections gone forward, Hồ Chi Minh would surely have been elected. Instead, Diệm staged a

---

[83] Fitzgerald. P. 95.

[84] *Ibid.* P. 111.

[85] The primary provisions of the Geneva Accords of 1954 are included in the Appendices.

plebiscite, which declared VietNam a Republic named, "The Republic of VietNam", with himself as president. So did Diệm stage a coup in which he replaced the emperor, Bao Dai, who had appointed him. This act, and the appointment of extended family to most positions of power was highly resented. Prime Minister/President Diệm's oldest brother was Archbishop of Hue, and was a very powerful man. GVN officials and ARVN officers had to convert to Roman Catholicism and prove they had attended Mass weekly in order to hold their office. Religion became a test of loyalty to the ruling family, enraging the traditionalists and nationalists. [86]

Fitzgerald says Diệm ran a government functioning in direct opposition to the institutions of the GVN.[87] Military commanders and high-ranking officials were appointed based on their loyalty and not their competence. He did not govern, but tried to be an ascetic Confucian paradigm that people would follow, even though his brothers did rule and their appointees rode rough-shod over the people. In 1959, Diệm secret police restored the guillotine to South VietNam and broadened the scope of political charges which called for the death penalty. Roving officials pronounced sentences without trial or appeal, and death came within hours of arrest.[88]

---

[86] Bui Diệm , with Chanoff, David. In the Jaws of History. Houghton Mifflin Co, Boston, 1987. P. 81-91.
[87] Fitzgerald. P. 269.
[88] Logevall, P. 692f.

Diệm suspended the Bill of Rights. His police arrested opposition politicians and sent them to labor camps, thereby alienating the genuine nationalists in the country. Bui Diệm, his uncle, wrote, "Every move he (President Diệm) made or were made in his name generated alienation rather than cohesiveness, isolation rather than interdependence... Nationalists who had been brushed aside became anti- Diệmist and increasingly militant."[89] Bui Diệm writes that the remaining VietMinh in the South sought support from among these Nationalists and other dissidents and, in 1960, the NLF was formed as a result of President Diệm's "family-run oligarchy and his brother's police tactics, political imprisonments, and murders without trial or charges. He further states that Hồ Chi Minh's decision in 1960 to move PAVN (NVA) troops into the south was made in response to these repressive policies. As of that time, he says, the countryside was no longer controlled by the GVN.[90]

In a general election, President Diệm won with over 650,000 votes out of 425,000 registered voters in Saigon. Afterward, candidates that had opposed him were quietly arrested by the secret police run by Diệm's brother. The U.S. knew all this, but did not want to question any election a Communist didn't win. President Diệm's government did no budgeting, but decided how much the South wanted and Washington paid. We put up with all this because the U.S. Administrations thought they had a strong man who

---

[89] Bui Diệm , P. 90f.

[90] *ibid*, P. 94-96.

would stand up to Communism, but he was fighting every faction within his own country except his own. In 1960 alone, the NLF assassinated 4,000 GVN appointed officials who had replaced the traditional village elders.[91]

Diệm feared and reviled Buddhists Monks, and banned their flags and religious celebrations, though such public demonstrations by Roman Catholics were encouraged. The Buddhist began peaceful demonstrations, which were met with widespread violence by the Diệm Regime.

A much-respected Buddhist Monk, Thích Quảng Đức, calmly set himself on fire at a busy intersection in Saigon. I have actually seen his automobile, which is visible in the background in the horrid, but well-known photograph of his self-immolation. The car is maintained as a shrine in a pagoda on the Perfume River west of Hue to this day. Diệm's police and army attacked hundreds of pagodas and thousands of religious people were killed or just disappeared.

Diệm's sister-in-law, Madam Nhu, the de-facto first lady, publicly offered free matches to any monks who would immolate themselves. Her only other public service was to ban the Tango. [92]

The prophetic role of Buddhism discussed earlier came to the fore, and everything changed. It became obvious that the fragmented South was completely

---

[91] Logevall, P. 702.
[92] Baritz. P. 91.

outclassed by the hardened, unified, militarized culture of the North. The U.S. Administration knew that President Diệm had to go.

As part of a South Vietnamese military *coup d'etat*, abetted by the C.I.A on the order of President Kennedy, Diệm was assassinated. Six coups followed in nine months. There were many more attempts, most of which fell apart from incompetence. On one occasion, General Nguyễn Cao Ky sortied in his U.S. supplied fighter plane to stop a march on the capital, but when he saw the balance of forces, he changed sides in mid-air. On another occasion two military commanders marched into the city simultaneously, mounting separate coups and ran into each other, ending both attempts.[93]

General Khanh lasted awhile, but only because he was seen as totally ineffectual. At one point he was carried around Hue by students who made him shout anti-government slogans. Most of the generals conspired to take over the government, but none had any idea how to form one, so coup followed coup. The first strong men to take control were French-trained and educated men, the second group were not educated at all. The South was flying apart from within. There simply was no government, other than that of the NLF in what remained of the villages.[94]

---

[93] Fitzgerald. P. 342.

[94] Bui Diệm . P. 108-109.

97

Bui Diệm says that the GVN failed because of bad leadership in South VietNam and because of lack of understanding in Washington. He believes that we had the opportunity handed to us to support democratic nationalists in the South, but didn't recognize them. We abetted the coup against President Diệm but gave no guidance or assistance how to form a nation (possibly because we did not understand the culture well enough to know how). From then on, the U.S. just wanted a strong man to control the army, keep order, and fight communism.[95]

Elections in a Failed Confucian Society

Here is another disconnect. Our Presidents needed some signs of legitimacy and some progress toward our stated war objectives, so pressured Saigon to hold national elections in 1967. The South Vietnamese generals who were sort of in charge were all against it, and the U.S. civil advisors were very nervous as well. The elections went off smoothly, and Johnson was pleased; however, few in Washington had any idea how the event was seen by the Vietnamese. Firstly, the candidates to stand for election were carefully screened to make sure no NLF sympathizers stood. Secondly, the mix of candidates in each province was chosen exactly to match the political views of the National Council. This meant that there was no chance of anything changing.

---

[95] *Ibid.* P. 112-115.

Most importantly, however was the cultural view of the election process itself. Because of their ancient philosophy, the people thought that if a government was so divided that it needed to have elections, the Mandate of Heaven had been lost anyhow, so the revolutionary teaching of the NLF was reinforced. If there was no unity above them, chaos ruled. Fitzgerald says the villagers considered elections to be "Instruments of terror."[96] Far from unifying the country and getting them to understand a democratic system of self-government, it further fragmented the country. This is further evidence that we should not mess with things we can not understand.

Flawed Counter-Revolutionary Programs

In 1967, U.S. civil advisors caused the GVN to create the Revolutionary Development Program, which was a near copy of the political arm of the NLF. We were mimicking the Viet Cong. There was a school established in VungTau and a complex political indoctrination program was developed and taught. Bright young graduates were sent into the villages with 110 tasks by which to wrestle the villagers away from the NLF. The reward for the village, of course, was lots of construction material, tools, etc. from American aid. None of that ever made it through the sticky fingers of the GVN, and the purpose of the program was transparent to the people. It was not to make government work for the people, but make the

---

[96] *Ibid.* P. 441.

people subservient to the government. Some of the cadre ran away in the first few days. Many of them were taken away from their jobs by local ARVN commanders and forced to serve as soldiers. The VC killed a few. None were at all successful.[97] It does show, however, that the U.S. officials understood early in the war the effectiveness of the NVA political effort.

Jeffrey Race was an Army Advisor to the ARVN in Long An Province, which was only a few miles south of Saigon. He writes in his book, War Comes to Long An, an account of how two sides prepared for and executed the war in that province. He shows that it was primarily a political war by the guerillas, which began many years before we committed troops and continued for many years thereafter. He interviewed many former VC and NVA commanders who spoke of things like solidarity and patriotism and showed their willingness to sacrifice in service to their beliefs. He also tells of readily-apparent corruption of ARVN and the South Vietnamese leadership.

Race's book gives a rare insight into revolutionary leadership and practice. He says that our officers on the ground had to make decisions out of an incomplete and even erroneous view of the enemy.[98] The province appeared to be pacified most of the

---

[97] Fitzgerald. P. 412.
[98] Jeffrey Race. War Comes to Long An: Revolutionary Conflice in a Vietnamese Province, University of California Press, 1972. p. IX.

time, but was actually constantly alive with insurgent activity.

He claims not to be suggesting a specific approach to insurgencies, but it seems to me that he does so very powerfully when he writes, "Man is moved by the need for spiritual values, a sense of power over his destiny, a sense of respect from his fellow man."[99] The book makes it clear that, at least in that province, which looked peaceful, was on the southern outskirts of the capitol city, and provided access to the rich delta of South VietNam, the preparation and conduct of the war was decidedly won by the insurgents and lost by the nearby Saigon administration fairly early in the war.

From Rural Development to Clearance

General Westmoreland arrived in VietNam in 1964 with the idea of following the old French tactic of pacifying small areas of villages at a time. He expanded the idea into a plan in which ARVN formations would sweep a large area of villages and Rural Development teams would arrive after them. Then, shielded by the South Vietnamese troops further out, they would then deliver considerable aid in terms of building supplies, tools, livestock, etc. to the villages to improve their lives and render the NLF irrelevant. General Westmoreland called this HOP TAC. For the first large operation of this type, the ARVN 25th division was moved down from its

---

[99] *Ibid*. P. 276.

traditional base in II Corps on trucks. When the trucks arrived outside Saigon for the beginning of the sweep, they melted into the city and went home.

The stockpiled supplies for the development portion of the plan disappeared into the black market and thus into GVN official's bank accounts.[100]   General Westmoreland decided that American Troops would have to do the job. I arrived "in country" in 1966 as part of the first phase of the big expansion of U.S. Troops.   There followed hundreds of thousands of U.S. soldiers and some Republic of Korea and Australian soldiers to take the fight to the enemy.

The General had decided that the villages, which had been the havens of support and supply depots of the VC had to go. I was stationed at PhuLoi, the forward firebase of the 1st Infantry Division, which along with the U.S. 25th Infantry Division engaged in large scale "Search and Destroy" operations which leveled villages and relocated the people into fortified camps, where they had no rice fields or means of support (discussed elsewhere in this book).   Many fled, leaving behind the graves of their ancestors and became refugees in the cities.[101]   I am reminded of my own family history, when, in 18th and 19th Century Scotland, the people were rounded up from the lands they had inhabited for a thousand years and driven into the cities or actually into slave ships.   It was called the "Highland Clearances," and the land hasn't recovered to this day – and, we still talk about it.

---

[100] *Ibid.* P. 361.
[101] *Ibid.* P. 458.

I remember being sent to Saigon for three days on sort of an in-country R&R and seeing the city teaming with people moving this way and that. Then, at night, the sidewalks were filled with those same people sleeping so closely together that one had to walk in the street to get by them. The NLF was deprived of the support of the villagers, but was the Harmony of Heaven being maintained for the people? It did give our artillery freedom to fire endless H&I missions (harassing and interdiction) to make the night more difficult for the VC and NVA, but the tactic gave lie to our rhetoric for being in the war in the first place. We were there not to give the poor peasant a better way of life, but to work our geo-political agenda and to address our own fear of the "Communist Block" and future "wars of liberation." Some of our leadership had even less glorious objectives.

I once was ordered to take my platoon into a village and build a playground at an orphanage constructed there by the (hated) Roman Catholic Church (with U.S. materials). Since then, several questions have occurred to me. Why were there so many orphans? Where were the ARVN or their own government crews? Did we really want them to love us or love their own government more than the insurgents? When were we going to pull out and abandon them? A major flaw in our thinking at the time was that we wanted to be admired for our military prowess and our kindness to the people. That is who we were; but, what we should have been doing was putting their own officials and their own army in that role so we could step back and eventually depart without things falling apart.

It seems clear now that we disabled every organ of government and military leadership in the country. We ignored their customs and traditions and tried to enforce our own. We preached democracy and then manipulated strong men into political leadership. We said we were going to build up the South's military capability and dumped huge amounts of the wrong equipment on them but not the will to use it.

We trained their soldiers for the wrong war and then told them to stand aside when we saw they couldn't and wouldn't do the job. We said we were going to save the peasant from Communism, but left her and him alone in their isolated villages or slums every night. We poured wealth into the country and made the corrupt rich and destabilized the rest of the economy. We acted like we were going to stay forever and run things as we did in Korea, but pretty well knew that the country was not critical to the United States and so we would in the end abandon them, as indeed, we did.

Clearly, it was this massive infusion of wealth into a tiny country that did much of the damage. There was no industrial base in South VietNam and the rich rice lands were defoliated and/or depopulated. The rice growers were by then in the cities working for the GVN or serving in the hugely-expanded ARVN. Huge exurban slums developed with no means of support. Millions had to fend for themselves in these places. I remember being in one, inadvisably, in 1967 and seeing most of the side streets and alleys filled up to the roof lines with garbage, refuse, and occasionally human bodies that could not be buried.

These people had to steal to eat, so trust and hope disappeared. With the massive aid to the country, it would seem that these people would have been helped, but they never were. Once they were inside the "protection" of ARVN, the development resources went to the countryside to counter the NLF presence. Unfortunately, that didn't happen much either, since the Saigon bureaucrats had no economic base either, and spent much of their time massively misdirecting the materials for their own gain and out of simple anger at the Americans.[102]

Frances Fitzgerald makes a fascinating point about this. He says that the graft and corruption reached epic scale, far beyond the economic needs or wants of the bureaucrats, but continued in order to express that anger. Likewise, the bureaucratic tangles of the administration and slowness of response were for the same reason. We were fighting the NLF and the NVA. The President of VietNam was fighting his own government. His government was fighting the Americans with passive aggression. There seemed no limit to the extent of it all.

One story is that a U.S. AID official had 40 garbage trucks shipped to VietNam in order to clean up the trash and refuse aforementioned. When they arrived, he sent crews to pick them up at the dock. Several days later, he wondered where the trucks (and the crews) were and went down to the docks to check. 30 of the trucks had disappeared and the rest had been stripped for parts.

---

[102] *Ibid.* P. 569.

There was no source of wealth other than the Americans. There were no jobs other than the titular GVN administrators, the ARVN, and those in service to the Americans. The GVN, says Fitzgerald, was like a parasite attacking its host. This war, he says, was more destructive than the fighting war mounted by the enemy.[103] There were no paychecks other than those paid by Washington. No one was engaged in labor that added value to the economy. There was no government other than that provided by the Americans and the NVA, and actually in both the VietNamese Confucian and Village traditions never had been. Their social structure had been destroyed with the forced flight of villagers to the GVN, the ARVN, and the slums. There was nothing that could last after the departure of American might and wealth. Nothing did.

The fact is, in the end, the U.S. did not lose the fighting war in Vietnam. We gained military ascendency at TET and turned offensive operations over to the South with the much-touted "Vietnamization" of the war, by which more money was pumped into a totally non-productive economy, making matters even worse. The political, ideological, social, and economic struggles were not engaged well or in time, and even discouraged; and the tactics we used exacerbated the problem. The collapse was complete, so the South lost everything after we departed.

---

[103] *Ibid.* P. 513.

Mao in his "Little Red Book" said that time is on the side of the insurgent. Other than the decision to attack at TET 68, I describe the North's philosophy as, "If it is worth doing, it is worth taking 1000 years." That is not something Westerners can easily understand, and is part of that clash of cultures about which we spoke earlier.

Murder in Camelot

Three weeks after the death of Diệm came the horror of the murder of our President Kennedy by an avowed Marxist. Lee Harvey Oswald, the assassin, had been a U.S. Marine, but went to live for a time in the Soviet Union, so the rhetoric of Joseph McCarthy seemed to be ratified.

Camelot died with the President, and an appropriately frightened, unprepared, Lyndon Johnson was sworn in as President on an airplane sitting at the airport at Dallas. We all watched it live on television - I never felt so sorry for any man.

To his everlasting credit, he got Kennedy's Civil Rights Legislation through Congress and countless other bills. He also shared Kennedy's anti-communist stance, but not his finesse. Johnson couldn't stand the idea of the impending loss of prestige of the US and of his own, so he went to war – a land war in SE Asia! This was the converse of all military thinking for decades. President Eisenhower wrote in 1951 in his journal regarding VietNam, "I'm convinced that no military victory is possible in that kind of theater." Then, in 1954, in a meeting with Douglas Macarthur II (of the State Department) he said, "As long as I'm President we will not go in with ground troops to VietNam."[104] At the same time, he shared the concern of Truman and the country about the reality of Communist aggression around the world.

General Maxwell Taylor pushed hard for military intervention. He had been a great soldier in WWII, Commander of the 101st Airborne Division, but that was the wrong preparation for fighting a war of insurgency. This was a different kind of warfare.

Then, he served as a presidential advisor, went back to the Army to be Chairman of the Joint Chiefs of Staff, then left again to become Ambassador to South Vietnam.

Thomas Ricks in his very disturbing book, The Generals, says that Taylor was at the beginning the lone military voice calling for the flexing of American military muscle in S.E. Asia.[105] H.R. McMaster, in his searing book, Dereliction of Duty, writes that, "When he found it expedient to do so, he (Taylor) misled the JCS, the press, and the NCC.[106] He helped to craft a

---

[104] Thomas E. Ricks, The Generals, Penguin Books, Ltd, London, 2012, P. 223

[105] Ibid. P. 225.

[106] The NCC was and is the National Contact Center, which came into existence in 1966 as an agency to help U.S. citizens find answers about the operations of their government. Compromising this agency is utilizing that agency as a means

relationship based on distrust and deceit (in and among the JCS and the President)."[107] This was a large failure of vision, loyalty, and trust at the top of the Military.

We used the means we had according to the way we fight; but, with no reachable goals, the measure of success became the body count of the dead and not the count of people who became convinced that their U.S. sponsored government best met their needs. That alone ensures failure.

There was a huge breakdown in dutiful and open communication between military and civil leadership. As an example, I must tell you a story about President Johnson and the Joint Chiefs of Staff.

Members of the JCS are charged in law with being the military advisors to the President, but Kennedy and Johnson had created a group of young civilian advisors and didn't much listen to the generals.

In 1964, General Wheeler and the Joint Chiefs were unanimous in their belief that President Johnson was running off a cliff with his VietNam designs, especially the concept of "Gradualism". They got an appointment with him in the Oval Office, and stated their opposition to his policies clearly and so were

---

of dispensing disinformation and propaganda instead of truth.
[107] H.R. McMaster. Dereliction of Duty: Johnson, McNamara, The Joint Chiefs of Staff and the Lies that Led to VietNam, Harper Perennial, Yew York, 1997, P. 106.

preforming their required duty. To the President's great shame, he paused in angered silence for long minutes, leaving them standing, and then unleashed upon them an extended torrent of profanity and degrading abuse.[108]

To the Generals' shame, none of them resigned.

A young major was there to hold the maps. He left the army and went to UNC to do a doctorate. This story is contained in his Ph.D. dissertation, according to Ricks.

In 1964, following his election, President Johnson privately said, "A man can fight if he can see daylight down the road somewhere, but there ain't no daylight in VietNam – not a bit."[109] In spite of this apparent pessimism, the President soon afterward went to war. Why? Logevall, in a lecture at the Miller Center at U.Va., answered that question, saying that it was because Johnson felt trapped by his own declarations and those of the previous administrations of Truman, Eisenhower, and Kennedy regarding the importance of South East Asia to U.S. interests and security and the quasi-religious fervor with which they had declared the evils of Communism. For 12 years they had made these statements and expended lives and treasure in their support, and feared the loss of credibility and honor, so followed the path of least

---

[108] Ricks, P. 257.
[109] Beschloss, Michael. Reaching for Glory: Lyndon Johnson's Secret White House Tapes, 1964 – 1965. Simon & Schuster, 2001. P. 35f.

resistance and of least national and partisan political loss and kicked the ball down the road.[110]

Apparent Deception at Every Level

And let's look at the deception, which seemed to have been carried out at every level. Lyndon Johnson ran for president on a peace platform, calling his opponent, Barry Goldwater, a "Warmonger". People believed him. "I want to be the President who worked to end war," he said. Then, in early 1964, Johnson began planning for massive bombing and commitment of troops in VietNam.

He authorized the use of U.S Naval assets to spy on North VietNam as part of the DeSoto Campaign. U.S. Destroyers operated along the coast of Tonkin in the North in a secret plan known as Op Plan 34-Alpha, which assisted covert operations against North VietNam, often in conjunction with South Vietnamese commandos – certainly a provocation, if not an act of war.

On the night of 2 August, 1964, the Skipper of Destroyer, U.S.S. Maddox, reported that his ship had been fired upon by Northern torpedo boats. Destroyer, U.S.S. Turner Joy was ordered to reinforce Maddox, and did so on 4 August. On that night in the Gulf, Turner Joy expended 249 five-inch and 123

---

[110] Logevall, Frederic. "Forum on Lyndon Johnson and the VietNam War." The Miller Center for Public Affairs, The University of Virginia. November, 2015.

three inch projectiles and Maddox launched 29 five-inch and 95 three inch projectiles at apparently "phantom" torpedo boats.[111]   John Herrick, the Skipper of Maddox, in the morning sent a message saying that the contacts of 4-5 August were in error, but the President honored the first message and ignored the second. In either event, the President's use of raw signals data and not the polished kind delivered by the NSA and other agencies was very dangerous.

The next morning, long after Johnson knew the report of the torpedo attack was very questionable, and ignoring the warlike mission of our ships, he asked for and received from Congress *carte blanche* to go to war. The President immediately ordered bombers in the air, which pounded facilities on the coast. The President got the provocation for which he had been waiting.[112]

The basis of blame is very wide, however. Note that this resolution passed the house unanimously and was opposed by only two votes in the Senate.[113]

---

[111] John Prados. VietNam: The History of an Unwinnable Wqr, 1945 – 1975, University Press of Kansas, 2009, also his article, "Gulf of Tonkin: Ambiguous Push to War", "Veteran", the Journal of the VietNam Veterans of America, Vol. 34 No. 4, P. 29-30.

[112] See the facsimile and text of the Gulf of Tonkin Resolution of 1964 in the Appendix.
[113] It was opposed in the Senate only by Senators Wayne Morse (D-OR) and Ernest Gruening (D-AK). Senator Gruening

Soon thereafter, a Harris Poll reported 85% of Americans supported war in Vietnam, though not with the benefit of the truth. Caplow writes that populations of modern nations, "are easily persuaded to support any war the government wants to wage," at least until it proves costly.[114] Maybe we ought to learn better.

So, the story has been told of how we entered the war, and on the morning of 8 March 1965, 3,500 Marines landed on a beach south of DaNang to protect the airbases which were by that time pounding the North. Protecting bases, however, involves patrolling well into the hinterland, and contact was made with NLF troops and the escalation began. Furthermore, the landing triggered the entry of the North into the war, and Hanoi began to send large numbers of NVA troops and material down the system known as the Hồ Chi Minh Trail and began to take over major operations.

When a platoon leader in VietNam, I told my troops what we were supposed to tell them, that we were fighting to protect the people of South VietNam from Communist aggression. It is interesting, then, that our Presidents never consulted the Government of the Republic of VietNam before making precipitous decisions. They were not consulted or informed when Johnson asked for the Gulf of Tonkin Resolution.

---

objected to "sending our American boys into combat in a war in which we have no business, which is not our war, into which we have been misguidedly drawn, which is steadily being escalated". (Tonkin Gulf debate 1964)
[114] Caplow and Hicks. P. 71.

They were not consulted or informed when he attacked targets along the gulf, or later when he carried out the long, intensive campaign of aerial bombardment of the North called, "Operation Rolling Thunder." They were not consulted or informed later when B-52s carpet bombed in the South in the long-running "Operation Arc Light." He did not consult or inform them (or our own State Department) when he landed 3600 Marines near DaNang, nor when he raised U.S. force levels to about half a million personnel. "When we want to do something, we do it!" stated Dean Rusk.[115]

Here is another example of was perceived by much of the U.S. as a perversion of truth.

In 1967, when I was in VietNam, a CIA analyst named Sam Adams was given a job to verify the South Vietnamese Government's intelligence estimate of enemy troop strength operating in their country.

Adams traveled widely in South VietNam, far beyond Westmoreland's headquarters and found captured enemy documents regarding procurement of food that he claimed showed that enemy strength was not 245,000 as was claimed by the South Vietnamese Military, but over half a million.[116]

---

[115] Bui Diệm . P. 130, 153.

[116] C. Michael C. Hiam. Who the Hell are We Fighting" The Story of Sam Adams and the VietNam Intelligence Wars, Steerforth Press, Hanover, 1994.

By the well-known British formula with which they won the Guerrilla war in Malaya, we needed a 10 to 1 ratio of fighting men – here it seemed that we were actually outnumbered 2 to 1. This is to say that we needed 20 times as many men as we had in country to make the war winnable. This simply wasn't going to happen both for partisan political reasons and because holding the line in northern Europe against Soviet aggression was still the military's priority, and there were simply no more troops available without national mobilization.

Adams' report was suppressed and he said that he was told that his job was to come up with the numbers the President wanted so he could convince Congress and the American People to "Stay the Course."[117]

The intelligence community, however, from top to bottom, did disagree with Adam's report. Evidentially, the rations figures he had discovered included both combatant enemy soldiers and non-combatants. The political cadre, the medical people, the transport people were all counted. Westmoreland and the intelligence services disagreed with that count because they did not have to face them in combat. It is a proper evaluation. Adams, however did not stand down, but several years later collaborated with CBS and Mike Wallace of "60 Minutes" and made charges on television that Westmoreland was guilty of "conspiracy and deceit". The sensation led to the Pike Committee Congressional Hearings and later a

---

[117] *Ibid.*

libel suit by Westmoreland against Adams and CBS.[118] That suit was later quietly dropped, and both sides stood down.

Whatever the truth of the matter, it is clear that Adams and CBS did much to erode the confidence we in the U.S. have in our elected and military leadership. It was part of the losses of the 60's and remains in other forms to this day.

Misrepresentation and rumor worked its way down the chain of command until platoon leaders gave company commanders who gave battalion commanders who gave division commanders who gave Westmoreland who gave the President enemy casualty reports that people thought the President wanted to hear.

We were told that the North would run out of troops, but then never seemed to until TET of '68; and, TET erroneously convinced the U.S. public that they never would.

President Nixon was more determined to use military strategy rather than gradualism to end the war. He mined the harbor at HaiPhong. He attacked enemy bases in Cambodia with ground troops to the screams of people at home who had tired of the war, but didn't knowhow to fight one. He was not free of charges of deception, however. Most significant in the press, perhaps, were the Anna Channault Affair and the Watergate Break-in.

---

[118] Davidson. P. 84fff.

Richard Nixon campaigned for the Presidency saying that he had, "A secret plan to end the war." Being secret, he did not say what it was, but later it was alleged to be what the Press called "the Channault Affair," and many came to believe that it was treasonous. It involved Anna Channault, who was the widow of famed Flying Tiger's commander, Claire Lee Chennault. His planes flew in Indo-China in support of the Nationalist Chinese Government against the Japanese. She was a Vietnamese by birth and apparently well known to Candidate Richard Nixon.

It is alleged and believed by most, that Nixon, or at least his campaign, asked Anna to invite Bui Diệm , then the Ambassador to the U.S, to several informal gatherings of the campaign staff with Mr. Nixon. The charge is that the staff or Nixon, himself, asked the Ambassador to intercede with then President Thieu of South VietNam, asking him not to agree to any effort to end the war until Nixon was elected. Bui Diệm writes that he did no such thing, but in reviewing all his correspondence with Thieu, found two documents which could have been construed in that way. Bui Diệm thought the claim of the Candidate of a secret plan to be "electioneering fiction."[119] Whether it is true or not, the image of the American Presidency was in retrospect badly tarnished, and this became part of our cultural distrust of our own leaders.[120]

---

[119] Bui Diệm . P. 235-255.

[120] It is possible, of course, that Nixon's opening to China was the "Secret Plan to end the War." Also, Secretary Vance was sent to Moscow to attempt to link talks over South VietNam

In this superficial treatment of deception and how it changed everything, we must include the way the war ended (at least for us – the South Vietnamese suffered horribly thereafter.) Henry Kissinger, our representative to the Paris "Peace" Talks made an agreement with Lee Duc Tho, again without consulting the government of South VietNam. The agreement shockingly allowed the North to keep their divisions of NVA troops in the South and mentioned only a single VietNam, as if the south never existed.[121] President Thieu was, understandably, livid. This was a sell-out of the most treacherous order. Bui Diệm wrote afterward, "In finding their way out of the war, American leaders were not deviating in the least from the peculiar arrogance with which they found their way into it and conducted it." President Thieu balked, and President Nixon actually sent a message reminding him what had happened to Ngo Dinh Diệm in 1963![122]

David Chanoff. who co-authored the book with Bao Diệm , pulls no punches. He says, "Our arrogant take-over (of South VietNam) was not forgivable. We disabled the South's political development and forced it into failure. We did not treat the Vietnamese as partners, but as hindrances to our grander schemes... The way we left was an act unworthy of us."[123]

---

with the SALT talks with the USSR. (Bui Diệm . P.255.)

[121] Bui Diệm . P. 305f.

[122] Hung & Schecter. The Palace File. Harper & Row, New York, 1986. P. 376.

U.S. Government Studies

Throughout the war, the U.S. Government commissioned studies by private agencies to try to understand the issues of the success of the NLF and the programs of Pacification. Prime among these was the Rand Corporation of Santa Monica, California. Some of these studies have now been declassified and show the agonizing attempts for folks of our culture to understand that of VietNam. They also show clearly that good information regarding these issues was formulated and passed up to the U.S. Government and was not believed or thought important. As an example, here is an excerpt of a Rand report dated in 1965, at the beginning of the American troop build-up. It shows the core fallacy of the Strategic Hamlet Program and resettlement of people away from their ancestral villages. It was prepared in response to a request from General Westmoreland to study the evolution of a Vietnamese Village as it passes from "insurgent control to government control;" that is, from their own ancestral village to a pacified strategic hamlet.

Perhaps the most stark example, in the eyes of the rural Vietnamese, of the government's disregard for the local population while building the airfield was the treatment of one old woman. One afternoon while waiting at the airfield for an aircraft to return to Saigon, the author observed an old woman coming

---

[123] *Ibid.* Epiloge

from Go Cao hamlet. When she reached the middle of the runway, she stood there and refused to move. She claimed she had lived on this land for 70 years, and the government had taken her land from her without asking. Furthermore, they did not even allow her to remove the bones from the nine family graves under the spot where she stood. This was a serious charge against the government, as the Vietnamese, and especially the rural dwellers, revere their departed relatives, and their graveyards are considered sacrosanct.

Have a look at the conclusion of this report

They (the Villagers of have not seen any government people who have been truthful to them; therefore, the government should use a program designed to deal directly and fairly with the people. You must treat them nicely and give them service if you want to gain their trust. If this is done, then their children, brothers, husbands, and friends in the Liberation Front will return to us. But this will be a very long process.[124]

This report, and I am sure many others, signaled the cultural disconnect of the war and the counter-productive nature of our approach to the rural

---

[124] Rand Corporation. "Evolution of a Vietnamese Village", Memorandum RM-4552-1-ARPA. Prepared for the Advanced Research Projects Agency at he request of Commander, USARV, VietNam. April, 1965.

population. It also clearly shows the bankruptcy of the GVN to address the needs of the people. It is enough in itself to raise stark questions about our involvement in VietNam.

Tet Offensive of 1968

In 1967, Westmoreland had moved troops out of the enclaves and into the field, since the ARVN were not able to do much in the countryside. This was the period of the massive Search and Destroy Operations. These were startlingly successful in pushing main force NVA and NLF formations out of the populated areas and even back into Cambodia and Laos. The leadership in the North responded by triggering the third phase of the Revolutionary War plan too soon. The plan was devised in three parts:

- Assaults by the NVA to draw our forces away from the cities
- NLF main force assaults on the cities, ARVN, air bases, communication centers, and so forth, but not U.S. installations.
- Set-piece battle to take Khe Sanh as the show-prize to the South and North and to the world, for such had ended the war against the French after Dien Bien Phu.[125]

The TET Offensive was a trauma to the people of the Vietnamese cities and, more importantly, it was a significant watershed event in the perception of the

---

[125] Davidson, P. 99f.

war by people in the U.S. Since the President had misrepresented the war to the people for years, we were shocked by the enemy's ability to hit hundreds of locations in the South simultaneously.

It was a bloody battle, but it was a battle our military was designed to win, and we won it - big time. Tet 68 was in large part the end of the military arm of the NLF, and thereafter the NVA carried the brunt of battle.

Furthermore, it was the result of an erroneous evaluation of the South by the North. The NLF strength was in the disenfranchised, ignored, economically devastated countryside. The cities were by then full of people who were dependent on the GVN and the U.S. for their welfare and way of life. The gamble that these city people would revolt, or that the ARVN would change sides was a major and costly error.

General Giap and Hồ Chi Minh were quick to understand that they had been soundly beaten on the battlefield, but not in the American Press. Thereafter, they did whatever they could to feed the media frenzy in the U.S. and exploit the short patience and rising anger of the American People.

Unfortunately, when the press reported and commented on TET, it became obvious that we had been systematically mislead by our own leadership. We had been told that the war wasn't really a war and that it was going well (actually, it was on both counts at that time), but suddenly, the bleeding and dying broke out on television and the American Public was truly shocked.

The Press also made it appear that we were being defeated militarily, although that was very much the wrong conclusion. Along with the Phoenix Program, which slowed recovery of the NLF from their TET disaster, the enemy's option for guerrilla warfare, (their first phase) was severely reduced. The major battles thereafter were more conventional battles of North Vietnamese Regulars crossing the border in large formations.

We knew how to fight that kind of war, but Johnson was finished along with our country's trust and confidence in our leadership, and this has effected my generation, and the Baby Boomers which followed, ever since. I remember the President's statement at a news conference well, having seen it on television. He said he would not use one minute of his time on partisan political pursuits when the war was still raging. He couldn't tell the truth even when admitting the truth.

Failures at Home

"The buck stops here" was the sign on Harry Truman's desk. General Davidson summarizes the reasons why we lost the war in VietNam with one phrase, "One man, Lyndon B. Johnson, provided war leadership which was grossly inept and tragically inadequate." He makes it even worse when he states that the war was managed for his two real aims, and they were not the freedom from oppression of the Vietnamese people, or even Kennedy's intent to stop the spread of wars of national liberation and Communism. General Davidson, who was a true soldier and war hero from WWII, Korea, and VietNam and who was highly placed in military intelligence, says that Johnson's true war aims were his own re-election and his legacy as architect of the "Great Society" in the pattern of FDR.

This, he says, is the only logical interpretation of his failed strategy of gradualism. It is why he refused to ask for a Declaration of War. Davidson believes that the President didn't reform the draft system because a reform would place his crony's sons at risk. He never let people know what he was doing so as not to arouse the electorate. He engineered the advice he wanted. He shackled Westmoreland to certain activities, targets, and areas of operations to keep the conflict under his management and out of the papers. He had no measureable war objectives for the military to reach, He refused to listen to his JCS. He gave away initiative to the enemy and never wondered what the strategy of the enemy might be. What strategy we had was not based on a coherent plan to counter the strategy of the enemy, but rather was based on the personal idiosyncrasies of the President and perceived needs of domestic politics.[126] Wow. I wonder what Davidson really thought of President Johnson...

---

[126] Davidson. P. 143 – 147.

Here is another big issue. U.S. Personnel strength in VietNam was determined not by the number needed to do the job, but by the number the military could provide without calling up the reserves or moving out of Germany, where Communism was also being confronted.

President Johnson refused to call up the Reserves, which are an integral part of the military. Instead, he used the draft to fill the ranks of units as people rotated home. This was an entirely political decision. He did not want to look bad or make the public concerned about his little war. He did not want the democrats (or himself) to loose the next election. As our soldiers reached the end of their enlistments or tours, they were replaced by inexperienced soldiers flown into the country who had not been together before arrival and were now led by officers and NCOs they had never seen and did not trust, and *vice-versa*.

It was certainly true of my unit. We trained together, traveled to the war together by troop ship, and operated together in-country. When soldiers became eligible for return home for whatever reason, they were replaced with young inexperienced personnel from the U.S. The result was that in a year, no one coming in, officer or enlisted knew or had confidence in anyone else.

This constant churning of personnel also meant that by the time a man was functioning well, he rotated home; and, replacements die at a much higher rate than experienced soldiers. General Palmer cites the refusals of President Johnson to mobilize, call up reserves, extend tours in VietNam, and to extend enlistments as the chief personnel mistakes we made in the VietNam War.[127]   If the reserves had been called up, men and their officers could have been deployed as trained units and this would have been avoided.   Trained soldiers fighting with units and officers they know are much more likely to survive in a combat area, so the decisions made by the President cost a lot of U.S. lives.

It is also very likely that the civil unrest at home would have been much less had the draft not poisoned the debate.   Cases in point are the wars in Afghanistan and Iraq – no draftees and no demonstrations in the streets.   (Although, clearly to me, there should have been.)

General Davidson and others have outlined detailed strategies which might have won the war, but that doesn't mean they would have been followed. Davidson, especially, has a great deal of detail in his retrospective and gives the levels of manpower, money, time, and political will it would have taken to do the job.   He concludes that no president could hear such a presentation and believe he should go to war in VietNam; and, then he was stunned to learn that just such a strategy had been formulated and presented to President Johnson by no less a soldier than General Wheeler in June of 1965.   The eminent General said that it would take a declaration of war, one million men for six years, and a major commitment for another fifty.   Still, the President

---

[127] *Ibid,* Pg. 169

pursued the war, Davidson suggests, because of his own personal objectives.[128]

The credibility of the American Government suffered a huge loss with the theft and publication of the "Pentagon Papers" by Daniel Ellsberg. These documents reported top-secret studies, contracted by the Pentagon, that showed that the government had been lying to the US public in all stages of the war. Here is a quotation: (The Johnson Administration) "Systematically lied, not only to the public, but also to Congress."[129]

We are talking about leadership. I think of a leader as a person of wisdom who can perceive an idea and make it live in the hearts of the people. For instance, Hồ Chi Minh, though harsh, was a leader. President Diệm , though harsh, was not.

And our leadership had no clue. We had no idea that in the North, tenacity and sacrifice were deeply imbedded in the people's mythology and heritage. We didn't know they could produce the best light infantry the world had ever seen, and that the South Vietnamese are very different from the North Vietnamese (see my historical sketch, earlier.)

---

[128] *Ibid.* P.185.
[129] United States department of Defense, "United States – VietNam Relations, 1945 – 1967: A Study", as revealed by the New York Times in 1971. Several relevant excerpts are included in the appendix.

Many critics of the leadership in that day and since are far harder on them then this. Edward Widmer writes, "It is worth pausing for a moment to contemplate how a group of patriotic leaders could have inflicted so much harm so quickly on the World Order."[130]

Classical Wisdom of Warfare

Assuming that there was a legitimate enemy in VietNam, there were places to look for guidance. None of the whiz kids gathered around Presidents Kennedy or Johnson took seriously Clauswitz or the classical Principals of War. From my own memory of my military training and knowledge of the war, here is how I see these classical principles as they were not applied in VietNam:

Objective – a military force needs a clear reason to fight and a clear object to achieve, which will be understood to guide operations, and by which we will know when we have won. In VietNam, the idea of "gradualism", so bemoaned by General Wheeler (above) undermined this concept. One day the goal was to win the Vietnamese Peasant and the next it was to bomb him to death. One day it is take that hill, and the next it is to go back to base. Finally, it became the body count,

[130] Ted Widmer. Ark of the Liberties: America and the World (Hill and Wang, New York, 2008). P. 317, speaking of our Presidents from John Kennedy through George H.W. Bush.

which is the antithesis of what we should have been about, which would have been to establish peace and prosperity under a quasi-democratic, specifically non-communist system. There was no way an army could win, with this kind of leadership from the civil authority.

Offensive – a force must take the war to the enemy in order to win. As at the Great Wall of China, Hadrian's Wall to the south of Scotland, and the Maginot Line in France, a defensive posture is a sure way to loose. It is also a great way not to have to know the enemy or the people. In VietNam, the system of large base camps with forays of infantry and huge use of artillery were variations on this theme, and a violation of this principle.

The Marine CAP program and the Army Special Forces were better, although the SF operations were among the Montagnards and not the South Vietnamese. It would have been better to pay attention to the British experience in Malaya, but we never even sent one officer to their Counter-Insurgency Warfare Center there.

Mass – a fighting force needs to achieve sufficiency of numbers to overpower the enemy where he is located. Most of the time, we occupied the large bases, referenced, and allowed the enemy to move freely among the population in most of the country. Artillery lighting up the night and shaking the ground is no substitute to being with the peasant and insuring his safety and loyalty. Mao did say that the people are the ocean and the guerrillas are the fish. Likewise, we bombed the Lao and Cambodian border and west, in an attempt to stop infiltration. I once stood on the Cambodian Border and saw overlapping bomb craters in three directions to the limit of my sight.

General Palmer postulates that there were alternative strategies available to us. In his book, The 25 Year War, he outlines one that would have moved our army into position to seal the borders and developed a well-trained ARVN to move among the people in the countryside without U.S. presence to poison the project. The Marines, instead of being used in Army roles, should rather have been used in their role as amphibious troops on ships off the North in the Gulf of Tonkin, threatening the North and forcing them to keep large numbers of troops out of the South and well above the DMZ.[131]

My son and I travelled the entire length of Rt. 9 in 1999. This road runs east and west just below the old DMZ, and goes all the way to the Lao border. There, just short of the

[131] Bruce Palmer, Jr. The 25-Year War: America's Military Role in VietNam, Simon & Schuster, New York, 1984. P. 182ff.

mountains, was the Lang Vei Special Forces Camp. Early in the war, a Special Forces A team with about 300 Montagnards were positioned there in an attempt to stop NVA infiltration from the Hồ Chi Minh Trail in Laos.[132] It was overrun by NVA tanks and infantry rolling off Koh Rok Massif in 1968. There was only one survivor. No presence was re-established there. Perhaps this is where the U.S. Army belonged, instead of a few tribesmen, and later, no one at all.

Maneuver – we actually did do this. The airmobile operations learned early in the war are an example.[133] Maneuver is the way to achieve mass where it is needed. Unfortunately, we conducted these operations all over the map in such a way as to inflict damage to the civilian population rather than stopping infiltration. The Marine presence off the coast would also be a positive example. We didn't do that either.

---

[132] An interesting aside: Laos was once a powerful kingdom called, "Muong Lan Xang Hom Khao", which is rendered in English as, "Land of the Million Elephants and the White Parasol." This fact is descriptive of the "otherness" of these S.E. Asian countries about which we know very little.

[133] See, Moore, Harold G. We Were Soldiers Once…and Young: Ia Drang – The Battle That Changed the War in Vietnam. U.S.A:Houghton Mifflin, 1992.

Economy of Force – Under General Taylor at the JCS (later Ambassador), and Generals Harkins and Westmoreland, we built a heavy force with emphasis on Artillery with country-wide reach in Corps I, III, and IV, and Armor, which couldn't operate in the two wet seasons, and therefore destroyed the infrastructure in a few weeks. This concentration of firepower, with most military hunkered down, sometimes under mortar and rocket attacks, was completely counter-productive, as has been stated many times in this book. Exercising Economy of Force would have looked very different. It would have put soldiers, preferably ARVN, where the war was being lost, in the countryside, with our forces in reserve or along the borders to allow the South's Army to pacify their own country.

Unity of Command – here we failed, as usual. U.S. conventional operations went through USARV and the HQ of Harkins or Westmoreland or Abrams, but special operations S.O.G., etc, went through Taylor, the Ambassador, and the million-man army of the South were not under our command. In fact, if you can believe it – I have trouble – each of the military governors of the provinces had command of the South's troops in his area, and were beholding to no central authority. The President of VietNam appointed them, but thereafter, it was up to

132

them to fight, or not; to coordinate operations, or not.

Many of them had accommodations with the VC and NVA commanders, and only went through the motions.[134] I, myself, saw the South's military commanders using their troops to build and protect their commanding general's personal business interests while our divisions did the fighting. This in no way prepared them for "Vietnamization" when we turned the fighting over to them.

FM-100-5, the U.S. Army's current manual on operations, adds three principles to the classical list. These are Security, Surprise, and Simplicity, making nine principles in all. Security was a major issue and we did all we could to achieve it. We pulled back most of our troops into fortified camps, again surrendering the countryside to the NLF and the NVA. Surprise was pretty much moot. Everyone knew what we were doing and what we were going to do. From inside our enclaves the civilian employees and servants watched and reported. Simplicity was never something we knew how to do.[135]

---

[134] You need to read about John Paul Vann on this one. See Neil Sheehan. The Bright Shining Lie: John Paul Vann and American in VietNam, Random House, New York, 1988.
[135] Field Manual, U.S. Army FM 100-5, 1994.

Likewise, none of the Presidents' whiz kids knew anything about Sun Tzu, a Chinese General who 2500 years ago wrote The Art of War, in which he says:

> If you know the enemy and know yourself, you need not fear the result of a hundred battles.
>
> If you know neither, you will succumb in every battle.[136]

Hans-Hermann Hoppe offers some stunning insight into this failure to know the Vietnamese. In his essay, "Time Preference, Government, and the Process of De-Civilization: From Monarchy to Democracy", he makes the point that it is very hard, if not usually impossible, to make the transition. An autocracy or totalitarian form of government is what he calls "private ownership" of the government, land, and means of production. For instance, Joseph Stalin, Adolph Hitler, Saddam Hussein, the medieval kings of Europe, and a thousand others in history owned and directed at will.

A democracy, on the other hand, is a form of government and ownership that is controlled by the people. This he calls, "public ownership." He says that, "Only in exceptional circumstances... can mass majorities gain the legitimacy needed to transform government into public property" (democracy).[137]

---

[136] Sun Tzu. The Art of War, Edited by James Clavell, Delacorte Press, New York, 1983, P. 18.

Doing it from outside the culture seems even less probable.

Also from Sun Tzu:

> No town should be attacked which, if taken, cannot be held, or if left alone, will not cause any trouble.[138]

And, one more quote, which is very pertinent to the Johnson Administration and its decisions regarding VietNam, is:

> Without harmony in the state, no military expedition can be undertaken; without harmony in the army, no battle array can be formed[139]

Hồ Chi Minh knew all this and integrated it with the systems of indoctrination he learned in Moscow and China. It was the source of the success of the VietMinh, the NVA, and the NLF. Hồ was very successful in phrasing traditional wisdom of warfare in sayings that can be remembered (much as was Confucius.) There is an axiom of his they often cited in the North about such wisdom:

---

[137] Hans-Hermann Hoppe, "Time Preference, Government, and the Process of De-Civilization: From Monarchy to Democracy", as found in the Costs of War: America's Pyrrhic Victories, John V. Denson, Ed. Transaction Publishers, New Brunswick, 2003, P. 471.
[138] *Ibid*, P. 37.
[139] *Ibid*, P. 30.

- When the tactics are wrong and the strategy is wrong, the war will be quickly lost.
- When the tactics are right, but the strategy is wrong, battles may be won, but the war will be lost.
- When the tactics are wrong, but the strategy is right, battles may be lost, but the war will be won.
- When the tactics are right, and the strategy is right, the war will be won quickly.[140]

The conclusion is inescapable that our leadership, both civil and military, disastrously and knowingly ignored principles that have been known true for over a thousand years, and that we were soundly outthought by the enemy. The outcome was, therefore, predictable.

---

[140] Davidson. P. 159.

Part VIII: G.Is and Families - Caught in The Crossfire

All along this build-up to war, there were other factors coming to bear. The '60s were a watershed moment in American life and culture. They were, indeed, a time when everything changed in our culture.

Upheavals at Home

There was the Civil Rights Movement, which came to prominence and some success in the 60s, but along the way raised the emotions of the people of all races. I can't tell you who among my 57 men were black or Hispanic. I couldn't have told you at the time without looking, because I didn't care. They were mostly all good troops. Then, Martin Luther King was murdered, and fires raged in 125 of our cities, creating the much publicized, but heretofore rare, racial problem among soldiers in VietNam.

There was also the rise of Civil Disobedience, which was shocking to the soldier far away. Baby Boomers outnumbered the Greatest Generation, and it seemed safe and good to challenge authority, one's parents, and the structures of society.

A huge demographic bulge of questioning young people ran right into the war and the draft engineered by their parents, and many said, "I don't think so." They took to the streets. So, came the Beatniks, the Anarchists, the Flower Children, the Sexual Revolution (I missed that one), and once the draft started, the anti-war movement on campuses all over the country, including tragic Kent State.

At the insistence of rioting youngsters, universities threw ROTC units off campuses, creating a huge shortage of educated company grade officers; that is, officers better prepared to think critically. This loss had horrid consequences. Accelerated OCS programs and commissioning of experienced NCOs soldiers lowered the educational level of company grade commissioned officers. Taking of NCOs out of the ranks left lieutenants, such as myself, without experienced assistance in leading troops.

Things changed very quickly at home, so our men returned to a country that had much changed while they were in VietNam. Many felt that they no longer belonged.

Combat Losses

But, the elephant had begun to stomp its way through the jungle of SE Asia. So, we need to talk about its effect on our military personnel and families. Here are some interesting data on our veterans:

- Of 27 million military aged men in the country;

- Only 6% served in VietNam.
- 58,202 died, including 1 female nurse killed by enemy action.[141]
- Of those killed, only 39% were of voting age.
- 303,704 were wounded seriously enough to require hospitalization. Twice that number were injured less seriously.

For every combat death there was an extended family which wept, and were forever changed. For every wound of the body, there were 100 of the soul. Richard Gabriel reports in, <u>No more Heroes: Madness and Psychiatry in War</u> that, "Given enough time in combat, every soldier will eventually suffer a mental collapse."[142]

Monsters and Demons

You know Homer's <u>Odyssey</u>, of course. Think of Odysseus struggling with one of the monsters. Cut off one head, and two appear.

This epic is the tale of the return from the Trojan War, or more generally, the return of soldiers from any war. It takes half a lifetime. On the way, you have to pass multiplying monsters and demons, and when you get

---

[141] 110,000 soldiers of the French Expeditionary Forces died in S.E. Asia before we entered the war.
[142] Caplow and Hicks. P. 130.

home, your house has been taken over, and your wife is being auctioned to the highest bidder.

Most of us adjusted.

Some of us are better men for the experience.

A few have not been successful.

All have to deal in some degree with a few or even most of these monsters.

I must say that these issues were and are not nearly as acute among personnel who stayed in the military – they had a supportive culture. Others did not.

Here are the monsters which VietNam Veterans passed, or for some, didn't pass. All are very much a part of the cultural legacy of Vietnam.

Psychic Stress (PTSD)

I have a friend who served as a fellow officer in the same battalion in VietNam who jumped at shadows or sounds, at least until he died a year ago this month of no discoverable cause. Another, a Marine Rifle Platoon Leader in I Corps with whom I sometimes lead classes on these topics, is spooked by tree lines and open areas to this day. These are mild reactions to a year of dire stress almost half a century ago.

Others have much more severe cases of what is now called PTSD, or "Post Traumatic Stress Disorder". This condition has many forms, depending on the nature and horror of the causal events, the duration of the stress, and I think the maturity of the individual soldiers at the time. The ingrained memories of these occurrences are monsters and demons which trigger responses to this day. Here are some of them.[143]

Chronic Anxiety and flashbacks: Chronic anxiety is a state of ongoing nervous tension. It can happen when it gets dark and the response is due to deep memories of peril and of the unknown. It can happen when going out of the house and there are lots of hiding places around you, like trees and wood lines. It can happen when staying home and one can't see a clear field of fire. Flashbacks usually occur with some kind of stimulus which triggers a stark ingrained memory. This can happen in the middle of a crowd when touched unexpectedly, or when a truck backfires, or the TV comes on unexpectedly.

One trigger for many of us is the sound of a two bladed helicopter, such as the UH1 series Huey. The tips of the rotating wings break the sound barrier when advancing in the direction of flight, making the characteristic sound of that

[143] Thomas Williams. Post-Traumatic Stress Disorders: a Handbook for Clinicians The Disabled American Veterans, Cincinnati, 1987.

war. The sound of a Huey would bring tears to my eyes until I was 50 years old. For others, the response comes with lack of sound, like the absolute quiet before all hell breaks loose.

A lot of study has been done on PTSD because it is an issue with soldiers returning from any such horror, but also because it is experienced by police, firefighters, and civilians subjected to a particular disturbing event or chain of events. I read in "USA Today" that psychologists have speculated that Jackie Kennedy suffered from PTSD after being splattered with her husband's brain matter and blood and holding his head on that horrible day in Dallas.[144]

Sleep Disturbances and Nightmares: These are the nocturnal manifestations of the above. Some veterans dread the night and are unable to sleep except fitfully or with self-medication. For others, the Technicolor dreams exhibit psychedelic quality and reach a depth of horror beyond creation by Hollywood.

After a knee replacement that didn't go well, I was put on a strong pain killer for weeks. As time went on, I began to have severely anxious dreams. In exhaustion, I would fall asleep, to find myself in a dream-like jungle, with very strangely shaped S.E. Asian flora and dripping moisture. In front of me was a cobra of huge

---

[144] "U.S.A-Today", 6 December, 2014.

size, coiled, with neck flat and wide – swaying hypnotically back and forth. I found in my dream that I had to sway with the snake, unable to pull away. After a few moments, the snake would suddenly strike me in the throat and I would awaken, startled and sweating. Eventually, against my will, I would fall asleep again, to have the same dream – again and again and again and again – all night long, night after night.

Depression: When the adrenalin from the above drains away, and one is left with exhaustion and a feeling of failure and hopelessness, depression takes over. There is a common feeling among such sufferers that they are useless and an impediment to those whom they love. This triggers all the expected results of anyone who suffers from depression, including suicide.

Addictive Behaviors: People who experience these kinds of psychic distress often self-medicate. In addition, in the last stage of the VietNam War, very high quality drugs were available to the GI everywhere in South VietNam. This was the time of "VietNamization", when the prosecution of offensive measures was turned over to the ARVN, and U.S. personnel were there with no mission to speak of and lots of time on their hands, but a continued feeling of vulnerability. Morale tanked, and drugs worked to blot out the fear and boredom. Most soldiers are of an age when addictions develop very quickly. I have read that it takes only weeks for a teenager to become physically dependent on a drug that might take years for an adult. Many soldiers came home addicted to these drugs, and some continued using them at home to cover the pain of their monsters and demons.

There are other addictions, of course. There is alcohol and tobacco use, binge eating, gambling, and others, all of which lead to disease.

Violence and imprisonment: It is hard to change in-grained habits of self-preservation. Somehow war puts us in close touch with the primeval fight/flight responses and it is hard to undo this connection as is required in civilized society. In other words, these habits come home with us and are hard-wired thereafter. We tend to react without thinking first, for thinking takes a fatal amount of time in the jungle. Some find another whom their subconscious identified as a threat at their feet before they know what happened. Many have found themselves in prison as a result, and return to society even more damaged than before.

Not having to engage in close combat, I have mostly been spared this response; but, even I have had occasion to understand what it is like. Once, about five years after returning from "The Nam" my wife and I were asleep in our apartment in Alexandria, Virginia, when I heard a snap nearby. The next frame in this incident saw my wife crash about half-way up the wall of our bedroom. She hit the floor, unhurt thankfully; and challenged me, asking what I thought I was doing. I feebly told her that I was saving her life. The snap was caused when the heat came on, and a teetering clothes hanger fell to the floor.

C.A. Byrne writes that among VietNam veterans with any symptom or symptoms of PTSD there is a significant incidence of family violence with more than expected physical and verbal aggression. The two researchers involved state that 42% of these men had engaged in at least one act of physical violence each year and 92% at least one act of verbal aggression each year.[145]

Failed Relationships: Most of the officers with whom I served have had apparently stable marriages. That is not the universal experience, however. Dr. Jim Goodwin, a Ph.D. Psychologists working with the DAV writes that the spouses of many veterans complain that their men are cold, uncaring people. This he calls "emotional deadness" from the many ways a soldier learns to ignore

[145] Byrne, C.A, and Riggs, D.S. "The cycle of trauma: Relationship aggression in male VietNam Veterans with symptoms of Posttraumatic stress disorder." Violence and Victims,, 11, 213 ff.

the horrors of loss of friends and the dangers of the field. It is also related, he says, to the need to dehumanize people with whom they must contend. A whole language developed around this process, such as "gook", "dink", and a thousand other pseudonyms that served to make combat somewhat more bearable. This coping mechanism was designed to remove feelings from life, and that practice is hard to unlearn. Dr. Goodwin writes that many veterans believe that if they allow themselves to feel again, they may never stop crying. He says that they have an impaired capacity to love.[146] I found in Dr. Goodwin's bibliography a book by Figley and Leventman titled, Strangers at home: VietNam Veterans Since the War. "Strangers at home" – that pretty much says it all.

The young men in my platoon were vulnerable to dangerous sexual behavior as a result of stress and of the incorrect perception that they were unlikely to survive their tour. My men had a VD rate of 23% at one time. That is bound to have affected them later. Several of them came to me for permission to marry the girls that the local Vietnamese ARVN commander bussed in to hang around the main gate of our firebase for $2 a shot. I can't help but believe

[146] Goodwin, James. "VietNam Veterans' Readjustment Problems: The Etiology of combat-Related Post'Traumatic Stress Disorders" Disabled American Veterans National Headquarters Publication.

that this kind of disturbance in the life of a teenager would color his relationships later. Even more dangerous are the other monsters and demons that stayed around after return.

The Presidents Commission on Mental Health reported that 38% of marriages among all VietNam veterans failed within six months. This rate is much higher with those showing symptoms of PTSD.[147] Veterans with PTSD were shown to be three times more likely to divorce two or more times.

Failure to hold a job: When I was released from the Army, I had a job waiting. Actually my employer had given me a leave of absence for military service, and I was assured my old job when I returned several years later. Even with that huge benefit, I soon found that people who were junior to me when I left were now my seniors in job and pay. I was lucky, though. I had a graduate degree prior to service. Many, if not most personnel went into the service right out of High School, and returned with a very poor G.I. Bill and no prospects of employment. In spite of the military's insistence that it gives training valuable to civilian work, what does an 11B (Infantryman) do in civilian life? What does an artilleryman do?

---

[147] President's Commission on Mental Health. (1978). . *Mental health problems of VietNam era Veterans* (Vol. 3), Government Printing Office, Washington, D.C. P 1321ff.

These veterans also returned with baggage. This section outlines some of that baggage, any piece of which would mitigate against being able to hold a job successfully. In the workplace, the idea that P.T.S.D. alone is enough to make an employee unreliable, ineffective, and even in some cases dangerous, is often seen as reason enough not to employ or retain such a veteran.

According to the U.S. Department of Labor Bureau of Labor Statistics, one half of veterans alive today served in the VietNam era and of the ¾ million veterans who were out of a job in 2014, 60% were age 45 or older.[148] This tells us that VietNam Era veterans are still paying a disproportionate price.

Alienation

The returning veteran of any war anticipates a welcome home as is appropriate for one who has put one's self in harm's way for the Nation. That happened in WWII, for instance, when the country was truly grateful to its warriors. Returning from VietNam was quite the opposite. We returned in the tumultuous '60s, a time of rapid cultural change, and the Nation was just not the same as the one we remembered. In addition, as the war soured in

---

[148] U.S. Department of Labor, Bureau of Labor Statistics. "Employment Situation of Veterans Summary", 20 March, 2014.

people's perception, the veteran came to represent all that was wrong in the world. Everything was different. People looked at us differently, or more likely, looked away. We felt quite alienated.

Alienation from Self – Who am I now? We hardly knew ourselves after the war - especially the youngsters, right out of high school and then VietNam, who had trouble thinking they were the same person as before. Truth is, they were not.

Alienation from Parents and Friends – We had no common language with which to talk about things. The returnee's friends and parents just didn't know what to say. Often, friends were embarrassed by the fact that they had not served, so appeared to judge the veteran as a result, when in fact, they felt judged by our very presence.

Alienation from our Country – we felt scapegoated by the very nation which sent us to war.[149] The country was in agony when we returned and so distracted that we were

---

[149] The word, "Scapegoat" comes from eight Biblical texts, including: "And when he has finished atoning for the Holy of Holies... he shall present the live goat; and Aaron shall ... confess over him all the iniquities of the Israelites and all their transgressions, all their sins; and he shall put them upon the head of the goat [the sin-bearer] and send him away into the wilderness..." (Leviticus 16:20 – 34)

overlooked or even blamed by the very people in whose name we fought.

Alienation from WWII Vets - They didn't understand the level of constant threat in Vietnam. The major veterans organizations which were very popular following WWII were not accepting of VietNam Veterans. We were told by many of the "Greatest Generation" that we had embarrassed the country, that we had failed and lost a war. We were told by some that we were "pussies", and couldn't whip a little country of midgets. We served only a year whereas they had to serve for duration. We were told to go away.

The fact is, however, that the average G.I. serving for four years during WWII was under threat for a total of less than 70 days. There were clear lines of battle and relative security behind them. In VietNam, even in firebases, one felt surrounded by the night and Charlie was good at probing, harassing fire, his sappers adept at creeping through our wire. The threat level was not consistently high, but it was always there.

The ground soldier in VietNam was there for the entire 12 or 13 months of a tour. In addition, in VietNam, you did the whole time, no exceptions. In WWII and Korea, men were pulled out of the line at the first sign of problems and evaluated and reassigned to the rear or back in the U.S. In VietNam you left at

DEROS, on a medevac chopper, in a body bag, or in five cases in our company – in strait jackets. You did the whole time or you were carried home.

Also, in WWII, men came home to a joyful nation, not a conflicted one, and they went home together on a ship, offering weeks of decompression and comradeship. The nation welcomed them with open arms – it was just, well, different.

Criminalization of Veterans – Some reporters and journalists thrived on giving the war and our soldiers the worst possible spin. It was a career maker to report and amplify a really bad scene. Bad things are part of warfare, and people need to know that, but it is a different story to criminalize all veterans. I know of none in my battalion who willingly mistreated Vietnamese civilians. Nevertheless, to some writers, every soldier was a participant in My Lai or worse. One California politician said in the last couple of years that all veterans were mentally ill and therefore should not have the right to bear arms.

One man I know was a Marine rifleman over there. He arrived home, full of memories of the warm hearth and love of family, but his father met him on the porch and told him he had seen on TV what we were doing and that his son was no longer his son and not welcome in his house. The old man never relented. The veteran weeps even today as he tells this story.

Grief

There are many forms of grief. Some are appropriate and can leave us a better, more aware, more caring person. Some are chronic. Some are an illness. All these are evident in most VietNam veterans.

Loss of self – The identity and the persona we carried before entering the military were lost, as were the military ones when we returned and nothing was the same. Many will say that down deep we don't change, but up a bit higher in our consciousness we do. Younger soldiers will have had to evolve into adults in any event, but the whiplash of war gets in the way, and the benefits of society seemed to be for others.

Here it might be good to mention that loss of romantic dreams is an issue. It is normal for men in the late teens to gain and loose relationships, as with a high school romance. Those are in trouble as soon as the youngsters go to college or to wherever they work. What is not normal with soldiers, sailors, marines, and aircrews is that if they are deployed, there is no opportunity to replace the lost relationships, and they are held onto for dear life. Dear John letters are painful when 12,000 miles from home. So is a return to find your girlfriend has moved on. Add to that the disrepute in which some held soldiers, and replacement of the relationship becomes problematic even after coming home.

Loss of Country - This grief refers to both the changes that had taken place while deployed (above) and the stunning realization that our dreams of a warriors' homecoming was simply not going to happen. This was not often real rejection, but rather the perception of such.

Loss of friends – Two things seem true to me. Firstly, relationships with friends one had prior to going to VietNam are no longer the same or often even viable. When I returned to my job with I.B.M. Corporation as a Marketing Representative, I walked into the big office in Richmond, excited to see my friends and co-workers again. There were 300 people in that office, and I had enjoyed many of them in years past. I guess I had fanaticized that they would all gather around me and welcome me home. When I walked in, however, every one of them looked the other way. Very few ever spoke to me again other than on business matters. None ever brought up my war service.

This was a cause of grief for many veterans, but it is not always rooted in rejection, as it might seem. Many years later, I was in residency at Virginia Theological Seminary, when there was a knock on my door at midnight. It was not a raven, but rather a fellow doctoral student who asked if he could speak to me. I invited him in and we sat down. He began by apologizing to me for his avoidance of veterans back in the '60s and early '70s, and explained that he had not served, and always wondered if he could have done so with honor and courage. The avoidance veterans felt from him, he explained, was his own avoidance of himself. This was a true healing moment for me, and I hope for him. That confession took courage. He had plenty.

Secondly is grief over loss of the best friends you ever had. Even though we missed the friends we once had in civilian life, the relationships of dependence and respect soldiers often have for one another in shared threatening experiences are never forgotten. They often end, however, because of rotation home (DEROS, or "Date Estimated Return from Overseas"), death in combat, or loss to the VA system somewhere because of combat wounds. This loss was the more severe since making new friends of that quality was unlikely because of lack of shared intense experience and opportunity. This loss, from whatever source, was a cause of interminable loneliness and grief for a lot of veterans.

Loss of Unit Identity – Troops deployed in a combat area do think of themselves as a Band of Brothers, and they hold a lot of loyalty to the unit that held them together. This was often a love/hate relationship, but don't risk disparaging the unit of another trooper. One returns home and looks around to find nothing like it in civilian life.

Anger, often misplaced

Combat is a unique experience. Veterans laugh at hunters who arm themselves to the teeth and head for the woods to stalk deer or other wildlife and think they are being manly. We quietly think, "if you want manly, arm the deer." The point is that combat is different from anything one has ever experienced. It is "beyond the pale," and often doesn't go well. It is a crippling, exhausting, anxiety-producing, fearful, dirty, bloody, dying business. The people and institutions which seem to criticize us in the midst of it or afterward draw our anger. Anger is often directed improperly, but it is real, and sometimes dangerous. This anger can be directed in many ways, and lasts well beyond the experience of war. It can be directed as follows:

Anger at the anti-war movement – A prime example of this is Jane Fonda and her trip to North VietNam in the midst of the war. She was photographed at the controls of an anti-aircraft gun at a time our pilots were in danger over the North. It was most unwise, and earned her the epithet, "Hanoi Jane". My neighbor, whose son served, though not in

VietNam, had a bumper sticker which read, "Jane Fonda, American Traitor Bitch." Many veterans with whom I have spoken believe she deserves all that; but, on the other hand, the anti-war movement was basically a movement to stop the war, and could alternatively have been seen as on the side of the soldier. The organization, "Vietnam Veterans Against the War" was one group of people who saw it this way. Nevertheless, I must admit to anger when I looked down on the Pentagon from an airplane upon my return and saw a million demonstrators. Now I understand the need for people to take to the streets on occasion. Free speech is a wonderful thing.

Anger at our political and military leadership – Lots of veterans hope President Johnson is, "Somewhere hot, sitting on a sharp stick." This is an example of anger, perhaps appropriately directed toward political leaders who got us into a land war in Asia and military leadership who had no understanding of the Vietnamese or concept of how to fight such a war. This anger cools, but is not forgotten completely. It should not be, since it could be channeled into productive investigations, such as hoped for in this little book.

Anger at the Press – This is another group that has earned some of our anger, but has a near-sacred obligation to make the truth known. More will be said about the third estate shortly, and you will see what I mean. The one place the press deserves our anger is in their interpretation of the Battle of TET 68, which was a huge defeat of the enemy, but was characterized by the press as a military disaster for the U.S.

Anger at our reception home - Enough has been said about this, and I think this anger melted away for some of us as we came to understand that our experience of war and homecoming was all messed up with the convulsive change of the '60s.

Fear

This includes first of all fear of Self – What have I become? One article I read said that nearly all VietNam Veterans could be charged with spousal abuse. Such is hardly the case and serves no one. It is true, however, that abuse is an issue. Remember my story, above, when I was startled awake in the night by a single snap.

Fear of failure - We began to believe what the culture seemed to be telling us about ourselves. Failure became a self-fulfilling prophecy, and the other issues some suffered did make holding a job difficult.

Fear of being alone, without friends or family – This is an obvious outgrowth of the feelings of loss and alienation and questions about the self. There was no one who would listen, no one who spoke the same language, no one apparently who cared. This was specifically a malady of those who mustered out of the military upon returning home. As mentioned previously, those who stayed in the military for a career had a support community of shared experience and purpose.

Wounds and Illness

Injury and disability – I served in 1971 as a chaplain at Walter Reed Army Medical Center, assigned to the major wound wards. Among the hundreds of VSI (an army category of illness or injury - Very Seriously Ill) soldiers with whom I came in contact was a young Infantry Lieutenant who had tripped a booby trap just a few days before. I saw his x-rays, and he had approximately 6000 foreign objects lodged in his body – shrapnel, gravel, pieces of wood, particles of uniform, and so forth. He had no face, no lips, no ears, no eyes, no genitals.

His chart showed that he had received 67 units of blood, since he was leaking as fast as they could pump it in. In prior wars, he would not have survived to reach medical care, but because of helicopter evacuation and excellent in-country medical facilities and personnel, many survived such wounds in VietNam. This officer was married, and was from the Maryland area. His young wife came to stay with him each day, and I would watch them beginning to work things through. Five weeks later, I saw him walk out of the hospital on her arm. These two beautiful people had their lives changed forever, but it looked as if they were going to make it. Who knows. I think of them often, and that was only one of many who haunt my dreams.

Walter Reed received a very bad press a few years ago. The problem was with the outpatient care, and I must say that their physicians when I was chaplain in that hospital worked their hardest on behalf of these wounded. The facility was over-crowded, though. I remember a one-room basement ward with 60 or more cranial injuries on cots with barely room to walk between them. I remember soldiers bed-ridden with bones being "stretched" with traction for a year or more, gradually replacing sections of tibia or femur which had been shot away.

Where are these people now? There are many tens of thousands or even a hundred thousand of them out there, along with their families or wreckage of families. The purpose of writing about the above couple and those injured is not to say that such sacrifices are never justified - sometimes, though rarely, they are. The point is that this nation has swept these families under a rug somewhere and forgotten them. This is a cultural issue which should be addressed. I keep saying to anyone who will listen that if this country doesn't want to take care of its combat veterans, we should not make so many of them.

Lingering illnesses with unpronounceable names – When I arrived at Oakland Army Terminal from Travis AFB, on my way home, I was asked if I had any physical or mental issues. That was my return "physical". If one said "yes" one was sent to some hospital somewhere there was room. If one said "no", one was required to sign a paper to that effect. I signed, as did everyone I saw. Then, a few weeks later, I was barely conscious with a raging fever that went on and on. The attending physician had no idea what was wrong, but just kept me going until things seemed to resolve themselves. I don't remember most of that time, but do remember hearing him tell my parents, "Who knows what he contracted over there." It was probably Malaria.

Others weren't so lucky. There was Malaria, Dengue Fever, Encephalitis, Hepatitis of various kinds, Typhoid Fever, Yellow Fever, Black Plague, Trypanosomiasis, Leoishmaniasis, STDs of unusual types, Hemorrhagic Fever, Meningitis, Lassa Fever, Schistosomiasis, Chikungunya, and more. I have no idea what most of those are, but some guys came home with one or more of them.

Then there are the lingering and late developing affects of Agents Orange, White,

Blue, and Purple, such as Alamyuloidosis, Leukemia, Chloracne, Diabetes, Hodgkins, Heart Disease, Mycloma, Lymphoma, Parkisnsons, Non-Diabetic Peripheral Neuropathy, Porphyria Cutanea Tarda, Prostrate cancer, Lung Cancre, birth defects in children, Lou Gehrig's Disease, hearing loss, tinnitus, and others.[150]

Guilt

Guilt seems to be a part of the human condition. I live with it all the time without being able to point to anything specific. I wake up in the night thinking that I could have done better in school; that I let my parents down; that I should have valued my soldiers more, that I should have this or should not have that. Perhaps some of it is true and I should beat myself up and make atonement if possible, but some is not earned. Guilt can be real or it can be imagined. I choose to treat the imagined kind in the case of veterans as Survival or Abandonment Guilt. Furthermore, guilt can be perceived as individual and as corporate. All kinds of guilt are psychologically and spiritually debilitating. The church wisely teaches confession, atonement, and forgiveness – accepting the responsibility, making amends if possible, and then turning it loose – as the way of growing out of it. It is a hard process.

---

[150] These horrors come from the web site of the Veterans Administration Health Services.

Real Guilt: OK, some soldiers (dare I include Marines) did bad things. Not many did, but some. There was a MyLai, and lots of other transgressions in the heat of or as a result of the horror of battle. Sometimes guilt is appropriate - some of us did things we regret and have no way to make things right. That is what is called real guilt, and the not being able to make it right leads to depression and self-destructive behavior. The way forward takes help and lots of time.

A variation of real guilt arises when a soldier believes he has been a part of something that was wrong or done in a wrong or ineffective way, causing needless loss of life. (See "Uncleanness", below.)

Survival or Abandonment Guilt: I feel an overwhelming pressure in my head when I look at the VietNam Memorial in Washington. My vision blurs and I feel completely unworthy. This is the well-known phenomenon of Survival Guilt. It is based blatantly on the fact that one person survived and another did not. Sometimes, as pointed out by Dr. Goodwin (above) this is aggravated by some action taken or not taken in combat or even a decision not to join a combat arm. In my case, I sincerely regret leaving my unit and coming home in one piece just prior to TET 1968. I feel that, even though I had reached the end of my tour, I had abandoned them and they got hit hard. I never forget that. I never will.

Unfortunately, many of those most helpful to the wounded suffer most from this condition. Again, Goodwin says that Corpsmen and Medics and the wonderful, dedicated nurses and surgeons of VietNam often agonize over the soldiers not saved, and in long night hours continue to this day to question their competence half a century ago.

Sometimes survival guilt is played out in self-destructive behavior, the veteran subconsciously attempting through dangerous driving, addictive behavior, or bar-room fights to atone for their survival and perhaps to try to set the record right – to become a casualty.

Corporate Guilt: In my church, we say a Confession together in most liturgies, indicating that guilt or sin is something we share together - that individual sin is the outgrowth of the human condition that needs to be held up, recognized for what it is, and transformed. We are individually responsible, but we are also responsible as a corporate body of the church, or a nation. It seems clear to me that our culture was not proud of what happened in the decade of violence in that little country far away, and our country wanted very much to find a scapegoat and move on. Thus many in this country blamed the veteran, whereas the veteran was only doing what the many asked of him.

Thus, VietNam Veterans came home alone and went immediately into the woodwork (or the woods). We need to get together and talk as did veterans especially of WWII. Their long trips home on ships and their hotels for weeks of re-engagement with home and family were opportunities denied veterans of our jungle war.

Uncleanness

The Old Testament concept "Uncleanness" never meant much to me before VietNam. In the Hebrew Scriptures we find that there is a price to pay for transgression against the law and norms of the culture. "Whosoever toucheth the body of a man who is dead... shall be unclean." (Numbers 19:13) "He shall make an atonement because of the uncleanness of the Children of Israel and because of their transgressions. (Leviticus 16:16) "If there be among you any man not clean, then he shall not come into the camp." (Deuteronomy 23:10)

This proclamation of the corporate spirituality and culture of a people that a person or persons are tainted in some specific way, so that he or she must be separated from the community, is instructive. When the VietNam Veteran returned, he was judged "unclean" by the culture for many reasons. He had blood on his hands, and the people who stayed home didn't want it to get on them, so to speak. But,

164

even if it were true that those who stayed behind were innocent (which they mostly weren't) and we were guilty (which we mostly weren't), there is something missing. Even without going to the New Testament of Christians, there is corporate forgiveness and reconciliation built into the Hebrew religious system.

"And the priest shall offer the sin offering, and make an atonement for him that is to be cleansed from his uncleanness." (Leviticus 14:19) Also, "In that day there shall be a fountain opened to the house of David and to the inhabitants of Jerusalem for sin and for uncleanness." (Zechariah 13:1) Then, there is the huge witness of the New Testament about forgiveness of sin and incorporation into the body of believers.

So, this country didn't put their professed faith to work, either in recognizing that we corporately waged war or that, even bloodied, the veteran was due re-incorporation into the community. The Hebrew and Christian traditions each offer rituals of re-admission into the body.

Furthermore, many veterans played into this failure by themselves feeling unclean after VietNam. We did things we never believed we would do, and we got it all over us. We felt unclean, and there were no cleansing rituals awaiting us.

Loss of Faith and Nihilism

Moral Order inversion - Religious Formation was strong in the young of our generation. We were taught the Ten Commandments and the Rule of Love of Jesus. We were taught that all humans were of value in God's eyes and that we were to be His active saints on earth. Combat and its training turn these teachings upside down. All humans are of value, except the Vietnamese. Thou shalt not kill, except for the enemy, who is not fully human. It is necessary to demonize an enemy in order to kill him, so the enemy is by definition evil.

Nihilism – Mahedy writes that the stories of Veterans with whom he has had conversations in the bush and on firebases, "Reveals clearly a nihilism so deep that it cannot but extend to religious faith."[151] In the section on "The Arts", I mention Johnny Cash's song, "Drive On," in which he sings about this nihilism, or the apparent rejection of religious or philosophical systems and the claiming that life has no meaning, so it "Don't mean nothing." "Shit Happens." This attitude is, of course, itself a philosophy, and it became deeply engrained in the combatant to the extent that friends and family could no longer relate to his system of belief, and the trooper became even more isolated.

---

[151] Mahedy, P. 141.

Failure of Civil Religion – William Mahedy, of whom I have already spoken, writes of "American Civil Religion" passionately. He was an Episcopal Priest and Chaplain in the 1st Air Cavalry Division, and after two tours, became a counselor for the Veterans' Administration. After interviewing over 1,000 VietNam Veterans, he wrote his book, Out of the Night – the Spiritual Journey of VietNam Veterans, in which he develops this concept.[152] He says that we Americans had conflated faith and patriotism to the degree that they became one and the same, and that, in fact, the first became the servant of the second. The young trooper was pretty sure God was on our side, but was shocked when he figured out that God took a pass on going to VietNam.

The god we took with us was the god of our civil religion, which had no power to protect or to heal. While not able to articulate it, many soldiers felt lied to by his upbringing, and lost all faith in God or Country. Mahedy says that it takes decades for veterans to re-discover faith, and that happens only if they discover the God of the Cross; that is, the God who meets us in the places of suffering and death, and accompanies us on that journey with forgiveness and compassion.[153] That God can

---

[152] *Ibid,* P. 158.
[153] *William Mahedy. Out of the Night: The Spiritual Journey of VietNam Veterans, New York: Random House, 1986.* Various.

be found in many religions, but is conspicuously present in Christianity.

Moral Injury

There is a shocking article posted by Robert Koehler, a syndicated writer for Huffington Post, in which he says that "During basic training, we are weaponized: our souls turned into weapons." He says this "opens a deep, terrible hole in the national identity" and "go(es) on forever in the psyches of the ones who fought and killed."[154] This is the new concept emerging called, "Moral Injury", which David Wood, who won the 2012 Pulitzer Prize for national reporting, defines as "The pain that results from damage to a person's moral foundation."[155] From the recent headings in this, my chapter on war's effects on the soldier, it can be seen that there are more categories than just PTSD.

We can't assume all psychic injury falls under the same heading, and we can't treat them all the same way hoping for some kind of healing.

A long-time friend of mine served as a Marine rifleman in the war in Korea. He has confided

---

[154] Koehler, Robert. "Our Souls Turned Into Weapons", The Huffington Post, 10/16/2014.
[155] Wood, David, as reported by Thomas Gibbons-Neff, "Haunted by Their Decisions in War", The Washington Post, March 6, 2015.

in me as his priest who also an old soldier, as his family tells me he has confided in no other. Over the years, he has told me the same story dozens of times about a child of about 10 years of age running toward him calling out "G.I, G.I," and something told my friend that all was not what it seemed. He shot the boy right through the chest – and the child's back-pack exploded. He knows rationally that the boy was sent, probably unknowingly, to deliver that bomb; but, he had been reared in the Roman Catholic tradition and in his heart he cannot believe that he could ever be a person who could without certainty shoot a child.

This is not PTSD, though this old Marine might have some of that. It fits more under several of my categories of loss of self, grief at what we find there, guilt, un-cleanness, and conflicts of faith. Maybe this new descriptor will prove useful, since it is the fruit of not just trauma, but the sincere shock at how what we have done conflicts with our core values. Georgetown's Nancy Sherman has a book on the way titled, After War: Healing the Moral Wounds of Our Soldiers, in which she says that for some, moral injury is, "Realizing that what you choose to do or not do in combat doesn't align with the person your parents raised."[156]

I am sometimes challenged in my focus on the war in VietNam, by people who say that it was

---

[156] Koehler, *Ibid.*

no different from other wars and its veterans are somehow weaker than veterans of previous wars. The answer to this seems to me to be that the moral injury experienced is in great measure inversely dependent upon the perceived morality of the war itself. WWII is remembered as a "just war", and its veterans honored, appropriately, as victorious soldiers of righteousness. We do not remember the VietNam War in that way, nor do its veterans have the ratification of the culture and the war's outcome to validate their memories. I fear, also, that this same consequence will linger with the veterans of current wars, although there is as of now no public outrage being expressed, as there was in the latter years of the war in S.E. Asia. That is partly because we have an "All Volunteer" military now, so the public figures that they chose their profession; there is no draft to threaten the young who choose otherwise; and the Reserves are being used to the hilt.

Unfinished Business

When I reached my DEROS, the last notch on my short-timers stick (calendar), The Colonel called the unit together, insofar as they were nearby, awarded me a Bronze Star, and shook my hand. My driver threw my duffel bag in my, or rather the Army's, Jeep, and off we went for an all day ride, tagging onto escorted convoys and dodging a blown bridge to get me to Camp LBJ, way back at Long Binh. Then, I was driven to Bien Hoa airbase for a flight to Okinawa, then to Travis Air Force Base, then a bus to Oakland, then a flight to LAX, then Boston, then Dulles, then Byrd field in Richmond and a shuttle to the bus station in the city. A bus took me a half-hour north and I got out, dazed, in the late afternoon sun, and walked into the Country Store.

A telephone call proved no one was at home, so I shouldered my duffle bag and walked the last two miles along a country road. When I arrived, my dog smelled a water buffalo, and not me, and growled until I got close enough. Then, he bounded and cried. I let him out of the pen, and he put his head in my lap as we sat on the front steps for hours until my parents returned from the U.Va. football game and a party afterward. I sat on those steps for the next two weeks wishing I had never left VietNam.

We didn't get the job done – As I sat on those steps, I thought I left my guys, I left my fellow officers, I left my mission, to come home. It was time, but I still felt I had let everyone down. There was unfinished business. Many times, I almost called the Pentagon and asked to go back. That feeling became institutionalized in VietNam Veterans as we were continually told that we lost the war. That is not a good feeling. We didn't get the job done, but then, no one could describe what the job was. We felt that we had failed our heroes of the Greatest Generation and we felt we had failed our Country, but the truth is, they had failed us.

The Disconnectedness of the Returnee from His Culture

My unit arrived in VietNam in late 1966. I had a platoon of young soldiers, probably only a year away from their high school senior prom. Before we even got set up, I received my first order. I was to take my platoon out, we knew not where, to find and recover the bodies of 200 or more South Vietnamese soldiers whose unit had been destroyed by the VC or NVA. This was not something I wanted these young troops to have to do – it is not something I wanted to do either. Thankfully, the wet ground forced the removal by helicopter, so we did not have to go. I wonder how many of us would still have been dreaming of our first act in country; and, how does one look at people who were not in the military, be they friend, parent, wife, or sibling, and come close to sharing that experience?

In WWII the nation was fully mobilized. People who worked on the home front were very much part of the war effort and closely connected to the fighting man. During the Vietnam War they were divorced. Most people at home went about their business unaffected, and had no relationship with the fighting and dying. There was no connection, no common ground, no similarity of language for a conversation when the warriors returned. As a result, we felt ignored, cheated, even blamed.

That, coupled with the nation's rejection of the war and the desire to forget, meant that the veterans met their monsters pretty much alone. For most of us everything changed.

On 3 April, 2015, I sat in the audience at the Miller Center at the University of Virginia for a forum titled, "The VietNam War – How we got in – How we got out – and How we get back in". One of the presenters, Ken Hughes, finished up his part by saying this: "Our American soldiers protect us with their lives – we need to protect them from our politics."

Moving On

William Mahedy returned from his second tour as chaplain with the 101st Airborne and began to ask the question, "Where was God in VietNam?" It is a profound question for a nation and a people who once claimed particular religiosity. In one of his interviews he records that one VietNam Vet said, "God checked out of the 'Nam' because he didn't like what was going down there. I would've checked out too, if I could have." [157]

The fact is that the god we took with us was a god our culture had made up. It was all about how good we were and how the little people of the world would admire us and do what we said because of who we were. It was the god that marched into battle with us, probably singing "Onward Christian Soldiers". But,

---

[157] Mahedy, P. 167.

Mahedy puts his finger right on it when he said that god couldn't deliver, and that God didn't go there to serve us in that way.

Rather God is available to us in turning loose of our anger and self-protectiveness. Sin now resides in our alienation. For a Christian, this letting go is best contained in a Theology of the Cross. We do not find God in our own power and presumptiveness – that just leads us into Iraq and Afghanistan. God finds us when we meet at the Cross, the symbol of vulnerability and openness between God and humankind, and between the culture and the veteran, husband and wife.

Once Bill Mahedy and I had an exchange of letters and of e-mail messages. I admire him very much, and recently resolved to get in touch with him again – to find that he died on 20 July, 2011. Time is running out for all of us. We need to get about doing what we need to do for ourselves, for one another, and for the Nation.

Part IX: The Arts and the War

The arts took a major turn with the advent of war in South-East Asia. They both described and contributed to the issues and turmoil of the '60s, and art tends to adhere to the memory of those times, and is part of the cultural legacy of the war. It can also be helpful in restoring our individual and corporate memory. Here I say a few words about some forms of art, most of which are beyond my ability to analyze, but all of which the reader can use as she or he might.

Songs That Spoke to a Generation

There were lots of songs of the '60s that were spawned by the war which are still remembered, and should be.

One such is Scott McKenzies, "If you're Going to San Francisco" (Be sure to wear flowers in your hair) is a song promoting the drop-out generation's gathering at Monterey, California. It has a very good tune and a haunting sound and well preserves its seductive message.

Bob Dylan's memorable song, "Blowing in the Wind", also sung by many others, asks, "How many times must a cannon ball strike before they are forever banned." It is a powerful song that has preserved a very strong anti-war message in our culture.

C.C.R's "Run Through the Jungle", and "We've Got to Get Out of This Place" by the Animals were especially popular with and remembered by troops for obvious reasons. VietNam is often called the "Rock-n-Roll War" denoting the availability of radios and music when in base camp. All of us remember, "Good Morning VietNam!" that howled out daily over Armed Forces VietNam Radio at 0600 hours, especially since it was made available to the whole culture in Robin William's film of that name.

Just recently, I discovered Johnny Cash's "Drive On". To me it is one of his most heart-felt songs. In it he talks about the nihilism of the soldier, who can look at his dead buddy and say, "It don't mean nothing," when it meant everything, except there was no profit in dealing with it at that moment, so you just, "Drive On."

Barry McGuire's "Eve of Destruction", also carries a real load of angst, and Simon and Garfunkel's, "Homeward Bound" is full of longing. Paul Hardcastle's later staccato sound of "Nineteen" mimics the sound of a machine gun and the sadness of sending our youth to fight in a jungle at that average age. There were lots more, of course: many of them very effective protests against the war and which are repositories of war memory, and therefore operative in transformation of our culture.

Films of the Era Serve Graphic Memory.

Likewise, there were many powerful films spawned by the war. "The Green Berets", with John Wayne was the only one that was released while the war was still ongoing. It was in the WWII genre of the invincible American and is expressive of William Mahedy's "American Civil Religion". After the war lost the popular support of the people, however, nothing else appeared for a long time. Then we got a goodly number of more critical movies. Examples are: "Apocalypse Now", "Platoon", "We Were Soldiers Once", "Good Morning Vietnam", "Born on the 4th of July", "The Deer Hunter", "Hamburger Hill", and lots more – some good, some very bad, but all now part of our culture, and all of which make the hair stand up on the arms of veterans.

Who among us does not remember from "Apocalypse Now," that most Conradian of films, the statement by the character, LTC William Kilgore, "I love the smell of napalm in the morning." I have 12 Casablanca fans in my house and I never, never look at one of them without thinking of the opening scene of that movie. Also, let us not forget The Ugly American. See below under "books" for comments about that powerful book and film.

Graham Greene's book, The Quiet American, was made into a movie (twice). The first one compromised the story by changing the villain to the British reporter, but the 2002 version, actually filmed in VietNam and starring Michael Caine and Brendan Frasier, was true to Green's story. Set in Saigon in

1952, there were two horrid atrocities, and Caine's character discovered that they were not committed by the VietMinh, but rather by Fraser's character, the "Quiet American", who turned out to be an O.S.S. agent provocateur. Caine conspired in his murder to stop this activity, though clearly from mixed motives – they were in love with the same girl. The message clearly is that our intelligence operatives set aside the high moral ground to discredit our perceived enemies. It is that old moral question of whether the ends justify the means. When this question arises with nations, there are huge consequences.

The Printed and Spoken Word Have Power.

Books abound on myriad subjects regarding the VietNam War. The range from the "I did this; and then I did that" kind of account that serves the writer better than anyone else, to more careful reflections on the cause, nature, and leadership of that conflict. A bibliography of the books I have read, or in a few cases only consulted, is included at the end of this monograph.

I shall, however, mention a few categories here and comment on how some specific works were helpful or interesting to me in my own journey home.

Novels by professional novel writers/observers: One is Graham Green's book, mentioned above. That book was written in 1958, so seems especially prescient. Another excellent but difficult book is Tim O'Brien's, Going After Cacciato, in which, "One rainy day in VietNam, a pleasant, moon-faced soldier named Cacciato decides that, all things considered, he'd rather be in Paris." You see where this is going. Philip Caputo in Esquire said that this book is about, "The profound physical, emotional, and moral effects upon the men who serve."

This kind of book is often more powerful than the historical studies frequently referenced herein. "Cacciato came alive for me one evening in March of 1999, while walking with my son along Rt. 9, just south of the old DMZ in Quang Tri Province. As we walked along, I could see a man coming toward me in the shadow pushing a bicycle. As he got closer, I saw with a start that he was a foot or more taller than the Vietnamese on the road, and he had red hair and a beard. He saw me, turned and fled.

Books by analytical journalists would include those by Peter Arnett, Philip Caputo, David Halberstam, Frances FitzGerald, and Tim O'Brien.

Books of psychological or theological import would have to include William Mahedy and Harold Cushner, and Thomas Williams.

Books written by professional cultural/sociological academics might include Loren Baritz, Keith Beattie, John Carlos, and B. Rowe. Loren Baritz in <u>Backfire</u> was seminal in the preparation of the lecture that inspired me to do this writing. One man to whom we should have listened before the war was Eugene Burdick, a Ph.D. political scientist from Stanford University, who wrote a story set in the fictional S.E.

Asian country of Sarkhan where the French Colonial empire had reigned.

The book powerfully makes the point that before sending aid to any such country, it is important to understand that country's people and culture. In the book, and the movie as well, the U.S. failed to do that, and the large foreign aid project failed. It is interesting to see in vignettes in the book incidences where small individual efforts did have an impact. This might be seen as support for the Marine CAP program rather than the Army's large-scale operations, but more than that, it is an indictment of our presumption of taking over a country to re-make it in our image, something we still seem to be doing 50 years later.[158]

Books by Political/Military Historians/Analysts would include H.R. McMaster, Robert M. Gates, David Hackworth, James Joes, Stanley Karnow, James McAllister, Bruce Palmer, John Prados, Robert E. Quirk, Thomas E. Ricks, Neil Sheehan, Bernard Fall, John Denson, Robert Caro, Robert Cassidy, Daniel Bolger, John Nagl, and a host of others.

One very pertinent observation comes from Paul Fussell, in his essay, "The Culture of War", in which he says that literature of war goes a long way to create a culture of war. He cites the need in warfare to transform "the ugly and shocking in to the noble

[158] Burdick, Eugene and Lederer, William J. The Ugly American . W.W. Norton & Company, 1958.

and bright." He cites the Time-Life volumes of WWII. "Everything," he says, "needs to be transformed into fairy tales of heroism, success, and nobility."[159] That is where we get some of our best and brightest warriors, of course, and we need them, but there also lie obvious, inherent dangers in the formation of public and foreign policy.

Accounts by veterans would include Karl Marlantes, Robert Mason, Tom Johnson, Harold Moore, Bao Ninh (from the NVA side), and James Webb (our former Senator). These books have preserved the experience of the VietNam ground, air, and sea warrior and much of their feelings of the time. They also provide a repository of history of sorts. We need to know what war is like and make sure it is worth the cost in lives and treasure before embarking on such a course.

Also preserved in these writings by veterans is some very colorful language of the war, not heard by those who did not have boots on the ground. In fact, that phrase is one of those so remembered. Everyone knows who "Charlie" was, or the "VC". "DMZ" is familiar. "Dinki Dau", meaning crazy, and "Didi Mau", or "move away quickly", are known mostly to former ground troops. Other examples include more nihilistic sayings such as, "Shit Happens", denoting a stoic acceptance of the inevitability of death and horror. Another is the ever popular, "It don't mean nothing",

---

[159] Essay included in "The Costs of War: America's Pyrrhic Victories", John v. Denson, Ed., Transaction Publishers, New Brunswick, 2003, p. 422.

previously mentioned, meaning the death if a buddy or danger to yourself was not significant. This, Friedrich Wilhelm Nietzsche would understand.

Less pretty even than that are the epithets used to cover horror. A "Dumb Shit" was a soldier who got himself killed – it provided an explanation as to why that soldier died and you did not - would not. A "REMF" [Rear Area Mother F*****] is a soldier or marine who worked at a large base camp and didn't get to enjoy "walks" in the "boondocks" or in "Indian country". A "FNG" is a "F****** New Guy", or a green soldier who is likely to get himself and you killed. A "Lifer" is a career soldier who might put his career over your wellbeing. "Fragging" is killing, often by grenade, of a disliked or feared officer or NCO.

There are a lot of these terms, some slang and some military, which are familiar to the G.I. and some civilians, which have stuck in the culture. I have assembled a Glossary of such terms at the end of this book for your perusal. My favorite, however, is the above-mentioned, "I love the smell of napalm in the morning", which I heard in a TV commercial only last week. The smell hangs around a long time.

The bibliography included in the appendix gives names of books by the above writers and more, and covers a wide range of issues and accounts of the War. All are useful in understanding how we got there and how the experience changed our peoples.

Poetry

Ours is an age of technical speech and writing – an age for the most part far removed from the disciplines of poets and storytellers. This has rendered us less capable of expressing deep emotion and describing events in a more spiritual realm. The horror, waste, and agony of war can be described to the mind in normal language, but it is best described to the heart by poetry. That is one reason songs of the war were and are so powerful. A second reason is they can be sung by anyone, and have a continuing, mantra-like presence in the mind. Likewise, many veterans resorted to poetic form to describe what was in their hearts and what they want to convey to the hearts of others. Many sites containing such poetry of the war can be found on the internet, and by all means, do look.

Something happened to me recently, which brought this genre into focus for me. I picked up a large, used carton at the re-cycling center, and it had a small book inside. It turned out to be a volume of poetry written and published by Kenn Reagle, who was in VietNam at the same time as was I. I began reading and went through it again and again. Looking to see where this vet/poet lived, I found it to be only a few miles from my house.

Looking back at the chapter on Monsters and Demons in this book, I find he is describing many of them. Here are some samples, with his permission.[160]

---

[160] Reagle, Kenneth. "No One Calls Me Hero," S.P. Amazon,

No one calls me hero
And a hero I shall never be,

But my year in Vietnam
Molded me into the person I am today.
That's just the way it is

P. 5

And,

I die one death at a time
Until my life is complete
They bring me home
But I cannot live again

P. 7

Note in these few words the depth of loss of self for a teenager who went to an unpopular war and came home changed into a culture which had also changed and no longer welcomed him.
And to see what PTSD feels like, just read this.

The early morning hours
Are always most difficult
Two hours into the night
And forty years ago
Just when I think
I control my memory
They sneak up o me
And the surround me
I am overrun again

P. 29

And:

2008, pages as indicated.

Every memory I have
Replays inside my head
Once they start
They all come back again…

P. 30

Grief and sadness comes out strongly in the following.

58,000 names
I look at my hands
I see their blood
How long, I ask
Until all are forgotten

P. 23

Loss of Faith and Nihilism learned as a coping mechanism in the midst of war carries over into attempted relationships for years or even for the rest of one's life, as has been discussed in this book. Listen to Kenn, however, state this in a very few words.

Nothing I say,
I say nothing!
Nothing I think,
I think nothing!
Nothing I feel,
I feel nothing!

P. 7

and,

She is hurting I know.
I don't know what to do…

185

Kenn, as was I, was moved to write in his medium by the invasion of Iraq and Afghanistan and is equally hard on the failure of our culture and our leadership to learn from mistakes made in VietNam. Our troops of whatever service deserve better. The following selection also mentions the bond that exists between veterans, who have experienced things they hope no one they love will ever have to see.

And now you ask us to believe you again
The call goes out to our children
"Your fathers proved their valor
In the jungles of Vietnam
Come now to the deserts of Iraq
They saved the world from communism
You can save us from terrorism"

I do not trust your
Destructive intimacies anymore

P. 28

I have talked to Kenn, and will do so again. He seemed eager to have some of the thoughts of his heart printed here, as he hopes it will speak to any veteran who might find his book. Perhaps he put it in that old box for me to find. Since I care about him, I was happy to note the possibility of hope in the end, as he wrote:

Peace comes, when love
Reigns supreme and we can
Value others as well as ourselves

Peace comes when we end
The war raging within us.

Neither Kenn nor I are saying that there is never a good reason to take up arms, we are saying strongly as ever we can, that we need to do so carefully, for the right reasons, for justice and concern for humanity, and with full understanding of the cost in lives and memory for all concerned.

Painting and Other Forms Of Expression

The first medium I want to mention might not be familiar to some readers, if, indeed, there are any. That is the medium of bunk canvases from troop ships that operated early in the build-up in VietNam. After major units were in place and personnel rotated into and out of those units as individuals, soldiers, marines, and other folks were flown into theater and the ships were again retired.

In about 2006, I was attracted to a lecture delivered under the auspices of the Jefferson Institute of Life-Long Learning (now called the Osher Life-Long Learning Institute at the University of Virginia). At that lecture, I met Art Beltrone, a local resident, who had worked with some film producers designing authentic sets. He had been retained to design a set for the movie, "Thin Red Line", specifically to recreate the troop compartments of transport ships during the Korean War. Art had heard in 1997 that troop ships were moored at several reserve fleet sites around the country, one nearby in the James River. He drove down and received permission to go aboard U.S.N.S. General Nelson M. Walker.

There, in the troop bays he found the typical troop bunks folded up against the bulkheads four high, and was astounded to see that there was magic marker and ink artwork on the bottom of most of them above the lowest. He surmised, correctly, that these drawings were made by troops on the way to or from overseas service. Further inquiry proved that the bunk canvasses had been replaced when the ships were refit for the VietNam War, and that these ships returned to the U.S. empty. This meant that the drawings were made by enlisted soldiers on the way to the war in VietNam. The VietNam Graffiti Project was born.

Other ships which carried troops to VietNam included USNS General John Pope, General Upshur, General William Weigel, General Maurice Rose, General Gordon, General Geiger, Benjamin Chew, Meredith Victory Kula Gulf and Point Cruz (small carriers), General E.D. Patrick (on which I traveled to VietNam), and others about which I don't know. A few of these ships also had the canvass bunk frames and provided Art some material.

Over the next year or so, Art travelled to Brownsville, Texas, and other sites where these ships were moored or in line for scrapping, and received permission to remove over 1000 of these canvasses. They are on display in museums around the world today, and some are on tours of the country. I have seen major displays (and Art, himself) in the Virginia Art Museum in Richmond and at the Albemarle Historical Society in Charlottesville. These canvasses are interesting studies of the anxiety, loneliness, and fear felt by these soldiers. Art and his wife, Lee, were able to identify several hundred of the soldiers from their artwork and invited them to a re-union, where many described what they had been feeling during the crossing. It is quite a psychological study of young soldiers on the way to war.

For a video by Mr. Beltrone explaining this project with shots of the ships and their history, see this web site:

https://www.youtube.com/watch?v=zDjGRRroPJE

There is also a genre of VietNam paintings. Some of these are easily found on the internet, but not much anywhere else. This art is often intensely personal and expressive of the soldiers very soul.

I have a painting which I purchased on a street in Old Town Hanoi – a 1000 year old riverfront town on the Red River. It is an original painting on silk from an unknown artist, which I purchased for $2, and which hangs on my wall today. It is completely "other", in that it is nothing like anything one will see in the West. For that matter, have a look at the frontispiece of this little book, which is a photo of Cham towers the like of which most of us have never seen. I mention these things here because it shows the huge difference in culture between this ancient Asian civilization and the West. This dichotomy, alone, should be enough to make war planners pause and ask the question which continually arises in this study, "Do we know enough about this people?" "Do we know enough about ourselves?" "Do we know anything at all?"

I choose to say nothing more on painting, since I am not the right person to do so, but this is a rich investigation not yet made.

I hope the above brief treatment of "The Arts" has shown that they together have preserved in our culture some of the turbulence and conflict, pain and death of that war, and that through them, the war has had a continuing effect on our culture. Next, we move to how our culture was affected, or perhaps effected, in the aftermath of those years. Later, we shall have a look at where we are now.

Part X: The Aftermath and its Effects on Our Culture

Our Presidents of the VietNam War era had some wonderful qualities, though each had his eccentricities and significant failings, and they lived under the compulsion of our history and cultural mythology, as did the rest of us. As a result, Presidents Johnson and Nixon each acted in a heavy-handed manner in VietNam to confront communism, gain respect, and insure his political party's victory in subsequent elections, with no understanding of the nature of the conflict; and, they failed.   This section deals with the effects on the U.S. Culture. That of the Vietnamese is unfathomable.

Failure of Vision

Our prestige plummeted at the carpet-bombing of a weak, pre-industrial country and at the humiliating loss of the South to the conventional assault after we withdrew. The result of our efforts to maintain our prestige in the world was a huge lost of credibility, respect, and even honor.

Then came the dastardly attack on our country on 11 September 2001 – the destruction of the World Trade Center and the people therein. We responded with indignation and embarrassment that anyone would dare do such a thing. Much of the world was at first very sympathetic, but again we responded with massive force in places and ways and against peoples not clearly at fault, and thereby lost most of the world's good will.

Again, we find ourselves deeply engaged in wars among peoples and cultures we do not understand. Once again, we thought peoples far different from us would welcome us as liberators.

Once again the battlefield is not what we expected. A conventional assault in Iraq was initially successful, but was not followed with needed consolidation and political wisdom, and we found ourselves in another insurgency.

Once again we thought a people of a different history would adopt our western style of polity. None of that has happened in the tribal conflicts of Iraq and Afghanistan any more than they did in VietNam. The seeds of democracy can successfully be planted only in a garden with a particular kind of soil, and we have trouble accepting that fact. Most in this country hailed the "Arab Spring" as a wonderful opportunity for those states to adopt our system of polity and governance, but how can that happen when there is no requisite history and experience of such? The result will be internal struggles for power and the emergence of more totalitarianism and less security for everyone.

In Afghanistan and Iraq, we found ourselves again facing a people who fight in ways we do not readily understand and to which we do not easily adapt. Our men and women in these wars preform well, but are out of their element. Anything short of total war will leave them exposed and vulnerable with unclear objectives, which are hardly possible to achieve. This is certainly an old lesson not learned.

Distrust of Political and Military Leadership

The very questionable Gulf of Tonkin Resolution and the terrible cost of the war caused the Congress to craft the War Powers Act, which requires the President to report to Congress; but, where went the obligation and sole right of Congress to declare war? It raises the question in my mind of how one man can commit young men, and now women, to harm's way in a foreign country. Oh, I know the rationale, I just don't like it.

In 1968 our political system was shaken in the Democratic Party fiasco in Chicago. One of my former soldiers survived VietNam, but was killed there in his own home town. Public trust and confidence in Congress plummeted.

A cross-border conventional assault in April of '72 from the North into Quang Tri Province was turned back decisively by B-52 bombers. This was total conventional warfare; but, after we left, Congress soon cut off funds for support of the South, which signaled the North to invade. They did. That decision by Congress also told our veterans that their sacrifice wasn't worth salvaging. We VietNam Veterans well understand how Iraqi and Afghanistan veterans must now feel.

In a CBS News Poll released May 19th of 2014, it was reported that only 5% of voters think members of Congress have done their job sufficiently well to deserve re-election. The results of the subsequent mid-term elections seem to confirm that contention. The issues are not all the same, but Congress and the Presidency have not recovered the trust and confidence of the people.

Again, we have made huge mistakes in the engagement and execution of wars in remote parts of the world.

Robert Gates was Secretary of Defense under both President Bush 43 and President Obama. In his book, Duty, he writes that he was stunned by the amazing bungling in Iraq, that seemed to ignore every lesson learned in VietNam and from the end of WWII for that matter. He cites as examples, failure to stop the looting of Baghdad, disbanding of the Iraqi Army, and de-Baathification of the government.

He says he was surprised that our military had forgotten everything they had learned about fighting an insurgency. Thomas Ricks, Pulitzer Prize winner, in his book, Fiasco, writes, "The U.S. invasion of Iraq was launched recklessly, with a flawed plan for war and a worse approach to occupation; and that the U.S. Army in Iraq – incorrect in its assumptions, lacking a workable concept of operations, and bereft of an overarching strategy – completed the job of creating the insurgency.."[161]

---

[161] Thomas E. Ricks. Fiasco: The American Military

Secretary Gates speaks of, "Crippling strategic and tactical mistakes in Iraq;" and our, "Civil and military leadership's failure to take even a minimally-adequate long-range view." He says of our legislative branch that, "Congress is best viewed from a distance – the farther the better", he writes; "Because up close it is truly ugly."[162]

In an interview with Chuck Todd and "Meet the Press", Retired General and Secretary of State Colin Powell said that we made huge mistakes in Iraq after taking Bagdad. He said:

> *Be very, very careful about displacing the leadership of a culture which has been around for 100s or 1000s of years.*
>
> *When you take out the head of a government that has no second level of support underneath, you get fragmentation, you get a quagmire - you get ISIS.*[163]

It is clear, therefore, that errors of both civilian and military leadership continue. They evidentially caused the mess in which we now find ourselves. ISIS had its beginning, we are now told, in the U.S.-run Bucca

Adventure in IraqThe Penguin Press, New York, 2006. P.190.
[162] Robert M. Gates. Duty: Memoirs of a Secretary at War, Alfred A. Knopf, New York, 2014. P. 579.
[163] "Meet the Press", NBC Television Network, Interview with Colin Powell by Chuck Todd, 6 September 2015.

prison camp where radicals got together and began networking.

They merged with former members of the Iraqi Army, whom we sent home in disgrace, but who knew where the arms were hidden. The result is a radicalized, disciplined, well-trained, heavily-equipped army which now calls itself the Islamic State. This could have been avoided. In fact, General Shinseki warned before the invasion that we were going into Iraq with half the force needed to protect assets in the rear of advancing troops, and he was fired for his insight.[164]

Secretary Gates cites the continuing lack of trust, understanding, and communication between civilian presidential staffers, the Pentagon, the President, and Congress. He worries about Presidents taking military action without understanding the long-term ramifications, and criticizes Congress for standing by and letting it happen. Here is how Secretary Gates characterizes Congress: "Uncivil, incompetent in fulfilling basic constitutional responsibilities, micromanagerial, parochial, hypocritical, egotistical, thin-skinned, often putting self and reelection before country."[165]

Remembering VietNam is a very good idea, since after half a century it can now be dissected and studied more dispassionately. It likely represents

---

[164] John Althouse. "Army Chief: Force to Occupy Iraq Massive", U.S.A. Today, the Gannett Co, Inc. 25 March 2003.
[165] Gates.. P. 581.

more closely the kind of war we will face in the future, but we clearly made mistakes - fatal ones. General Palmer states, The United States cannot afford to put itself again at such an enormous strategic disadvantage as that in which we found ourselves in VietNam.[166] It seems to me that we have very much done so, repeatedly.

Our military needs to do serious study of these issues, and our JCS system needs to be modified so that they are part of the chain of command. Some studies of strategy and tactics of the VietNam War have been done by the Army, but mostly those efforts have been underfunded and underappreciated.

Truthfulness is still an issue. Fred Hitz writes, and I quote:

> Political pressure to arrive at an intelligence judgment that bolsters a president's security policy is as common in Washington as the springtime arrival of the cherry blossoms.[167]

He lists examples, such as using the flawed belief regarding the existence of weapons of mass destruction as a rationale for invading Iraq and claiming that Saddam Hussein was harboring Al Qaeda training camps, when the CIA said otherwise.[168]

---

[166] Palmer. P. 210.
[167] Frederick p. Hitz. Why Spy? Espionage in an Age of Uncertainty, St. Martin's Press, New York. P. 92.
[168] Ibid. P. 93.

I was stunned by a Miller Center at the University of Virginia presentation called, "The American Forum", aired on 15 February of 2015. Featured were two Army officers with long service, Lt. General Daniel Bolger, USA Ret and Lt. Col. John Nagl, also retired. General Bolger has recently published a book with the very shocking title, Why We Lost, referring to the wars in Afghanistan and Iraq. He says that we created an enemy with an endless time clock, and that unless the People of the United States decide openly and firmly that we are ready to stay in a country pretty much forever, we should not think we are going to change anything except for the worse.

Surges of commitment will work for awhile, but the enemy knows that surges are by nature temporary. Mao said that, "When the enemy advances, we withdraw; when they withdraw, we advance. " Col. Nagl said in this broadcast that, "We invaded a country (Iraq) that didn't have to be invaded; we did it badly with far too few troops; and we did it with no post-conflict plan and no idea of staying to see things through. Douglas Blackman, the moderator, called the wars in Iraq and Afghanistan, "Nightmares of poor decisions."

So, we have once again a huge failure of leadership from the White House, from Congress, and from Military Commanders. General Bolger says that there needs to be accountability for these failures – there needs to be public debate on the use of U.S. power around the world. There needs to be firm commitment in Congress and in the countryside to stay a generation or two or three if we think we are going to achieve anything after military interventions abroad. [169]

General Stanley McChrystal was overall commander in Afghanistan and has since left the army (after a dust-up with the President) and co-founded a consulting company that teaches leadership. He says that organizations larger than about 100 persons become compartmentalized. They operate as if each part "lives and works in a silo," shut off from other components. "No one was ever criticized for not communicating", he writes. Furthermore, he says that the problem is still there. He believes in a concept he calls, "Contextual Understanding," in which the command structure's function is to give overall direction and all relevant information and intelligence to units. Subordinate commanders then should have freedom to exercise initiative and act on that data without fear of being second guessed. The emphasis of these quotations is contained in the phrase, "the problem is still there."[170]

Loss of U.S. Prestige in The World

And, how about the world's attitude toward and respect for the United States? Fred Hitz, in his book,

---

[169] The Miller Center at the University of Virginia, "The American Forum" Hosted by Douglas Blackman. Aired 15 February, 2015.

[170] McChrystal, Stanley. <u>My Share of the Task</u>, Penguin Group, Inc. (U.S.A.) 2013, as discussed by him on C.B.S. This Morning, 11 May 2015.

<u>Why Spy</u>, says that to Islamic People in the Middle East and elsewhere, we appear to be seeking their oil, invading their lands, supporting their enemies, and fomenting an alien, secular culture at odds with their religious and traditional beliefs.

He suggests that during the Cold War, we were the defenders of half the world against the expansion of Soviet hegemony; but, now WE are seen by most of the world as the aggressor.

That is not a place I want to be, but we again have gone into lands not our own and created problems for ourselves as well as their peoples. I am reminded of a two week trek in the Amazon I once made. Our little group of "adventure travelers" came upon a large mound in the jungle, perhaps 200 ft in diameter and about 15 ft high. We thought it could be some kind of burial mound, such as are found in the southern United States, but the guide informed us that it was an ant-hill and that it probably went down a hundred feet or more below ground level. That is a lot of very large ants. It would be the height of foolishness for us to have climbed onto that anthill and begun stamping on ants, yet I fear that is exactly what we do in places like Iraq and Afghanistan. The more we stamp, the more militants we make. There has to be another way.

Losses and Lack Of Healing
Among Veterans and Their Families

Vietnam Veterans felt isolated, and marginalized for 20 years. Many still feel that way. Veterans had to build their own memorial for those who had fallen. Homelessness and unemployment have been a concern. The GI Bill after WWII would pay for a four year college education. Ours wouldn't pay for books.

The recent fiasco in the Veterans' Administration Health System is a case in point. The cost of war goes on for generations after the fighting ends. Agent Orange related and other horrid diseases cripple and shorten the lives of tens of thousands, and of their children.

The anti-war movement, indeed the whole drop-out generation, caused a rift between fathers and sons and veterans and flower children that persisted for a decade. The passion of the counter-culture has faded, and we have a new problem, "Who will now ask the hard questions?" Where is now the youthful eagerness to build a better world?

Our VietNam veterans have been quiet ever since their War. Only with the advent of the wars in Iraq and Afghanistan have we begun to allow ourselves to be identified. Who shows up at the airports of our nation to welcome our newer veterans home from Afghanistan and Iraq? It is we, in our garish hats, standing up at last and trying to tell the world that these men and women, too, though they have given honorable service, have been ill used by our politicians and deserve to be welcomed home in a generous, healing manner.

Current wars have dragged on for a dozen years with no good end in site, but the lack of a draft has muted public outcry.

Furthermore, what about our military men and women on the ground in these two wars? They tend to be older when deployed than the men in VietNam, so more of them have families. The same units are deployed again and again.

As a result of these pressures, veterans of Afghanistan and Iraq are beginning to find themselves facing the same monsters and exhibit the same symptoms as VietNam Veterans. The incidence of PTSD among them has increased alarmingly. There is a chapter, above about the Arts, with a section on poetry by a VietNam Veteran. Here is one from an Afghanistan War Veteran. It sounds much the same:

> *Take our pleasantries*
> *your generalizations, good intentions,*
> *sweet words, and half-truths,*
>
> *Put them in a box,*
> *drape a flag over it,*
> *and bury it with the rest of the dead[171]*

---

[171] McClellan, Orrin Gorman, unpublished, but made available online by his parents. Orrin served in the 173rd Airborne Brigade in 2005-6, and took his own life at home after writing this poem in 2010.

Disaffection with the wars or the way they have been fought has been fairly quiet until now, but now is being heard. The motion picture, "Sniper", is one example, wherein an American fighting man is put in a position of taking life on a fairly regular basis. For some, this movie is a sad commentary on the fighting man, who apparently kills without compunction and without moral injury. Garett Reppenhagen was a sniper in Afghanistan who finds the film repugnant. Here is a quote from an article he wrote for the VoteVets organization:

> Unlike Chris Kyle, who claimed his PTSD came from the inability to save more service members, most of the damage to my mental health was what I call "moral injury," which is becoming a popular term in many veteran circles.
>
> As a sniper I was not usually the victim of a traumatic event, but the perpetrator of violence and death. My actions in combat would have been more acceptable to me if I could have cloaked myself in the belief that the whole mission was for a greater good. Instead, I watched as the purpose of the mission slowly unraveled.[172]

Some wars need to be fought, but most don't. We have lost as of this writing over 7000 service

---

[172] Reppenhagen, Garett. "I Was an American Sniper, and Chris Kyle's War Was Not My War," VoteVets, 21 February, 2015.

members killed and 50,000 wounded in Iraq and Afghanistan.[173]   Over 180,000 Iraqi and Afghan people have been killed.[174] This is not in the same ballpark as the violence and death of the VietNam War, but when balanced against any good we might have done, it speaks to our shame.

We need to be heard and lessons learned now before we disappear. The time to count the long-term cost of war is before it begins.

Loss of National Treasure and Recession

In WWII, the conversion to war goods starved the consumer market, but the war industry paid good wages, and there was full employment. Buying power was stockpiled.   The War ended the Great Depression, and after the war, and a serious issue with union strikes, we experienced a great surge in prosperity, which protected us from deep post-war recession.

During the costly VietNam War – almost 1 trillion in current dollars – half of the cost was lodged in increased National Debt.   Our political leadership chose guns and butter, and the cost of debt service soared. There was, therefore, no basis for economic

---

[173] Casualties.org, Iraq Coalition Casualty Count, Web. November 2014.
[174] "Costs of War", the Costs of war Project, Boston University, web, November, 2014.

gain after the war. This coupled with the oil embargo of 1973 caused a deep recession in this country.

We, once more, are paying for these wars by mortgaging our future prosperity. Debt service paralyzes our ability to do good things, and just wait until interest rates rise. One has to ask if financing our wars by floating bonds to China is a good idea, or does it poison our foreign policy and make us dependent on a (Communist) government. Again, the price of war is going to extend in many forms into future generations.

Damage in Combat Areas and the Vietnam Culture

Loss of life in South East Asia as a direct or indirect result of the war is estimated at between 3 and 5 million killed, depending on whether or not you include the destabilization of Cambodia. For those who think of such things, this is a heavy burden. It is a heavier burden for the folk of VietNam.

Material damage to the country consisted mostly of damage to the ecology of the region. This was and mostly still is an agricultural area with only limited industrialization, especially in the South. Jungles have been largely destroyed and poisoned, but rebuilding did not take an effort such as the Marshall Plan.

After the war, the victorious North moved 1 1/4 million people into the defeated country to take over all private and public assets in the South. One million

"Boat People" flocked to the U.S, reminding us of our abandonment of South VietNam. Some of these people became wonderful citizens of this and other countries. One example is Hieu Van Le, who washed ashore near Brisbane, Australia in the mid 1970s, to be greeted by an Aussi fisherman with, "Welcome to Australia, mate!" Hieu Van Le is now Governor of the state of South Australia.

It is also true, however, that some of the "boat people" had made themselves wealthy by diverting aid from the U.S. into offshore gold for their eventual escape should the South collapse. It is not surprising that many former ARVN generals now live in comfort around the world.

According to conversations I had in VietNam in 1999, men who participated in the former South Vietnam's military or civil administration and could not escape the country were made slaves for from 7 to 11 years. In my travels in the North in that year, there was still palpable enmity toward the former government and military personnel of South VietNam, though, surprisingly, not toward the United States. I was often welcomed with hugs from old NVA soldiers. Perhaps this bodes well for the future.

We arrived in VietNam at a crucial time in the history of the people. They were in crisis; their culture threatened. As much as we thought we were helping the poor peasant, the result was that we brought down the country around them. Our massive economic aid, displacement of the people, and use of defoliants destroyed what was left of their economy and their culture.

The current wars are much more controlled and have been of a lesser scale, but the durations are as long, and the cost to the countries and to their peoples are incalculable.

Issues Regarding The Press

Every evening during the VietNam War years, the nation sat glued to the network news, watching the horror being visited on and by their sons, almost in real time.

There is some belief now that as the Veteran suffers from his exposure to violence and horror, so does the public who watched it for ten years on television. That, too, was a cultural result of the war.

Veterans from VietNam tended to blame the Press for the failure to win that war and for giving massive coverage to the war protests. Some of this anger was justified, but the Press has an important role in a democracy. Citizens must have facts available to them in order to participate in appropriate ways in the formation of public policy. I do have concerns that reporting is not always balanced or fair, and have serious doubts when the press tries to interpret the news and attempts to sway opinion instead of reporting the facts.

There is another issue. Real-time reporting can have a huge impact on the military's ability to fulfill its mission. A great deal of intelligence has traditionally been gleaned from reading newspapers of the opposing side.

The North Vietnamese government and military paid a great deal of attention to U.S. papers and news broadcasts. The military and its assigned objectives can be seriously compromised by information gained from the press of a democratic society. In the totalitarian world, the press is tightly controlled for governmental, political, and military purposes. This is a serious impediment for us, but information is necessary for the citizen, so how much is too much? I note that from the VietNam War, graphic images flooded our living rooms every night, but recently, the access to the battlefield has been much more restricted. This is an interesting balancing act. Who makes these decisions, I wonder.

Damaged Military Morale and Capability

The military fell into discredit after the VietNam War. We did what we were asked to do, but we fought as John Kennedy (echoing General Omar Bradley) warned of fighting, "The wrong war, in the wrong place, at the wrong time" and this became the general feeling of people here at home.[175]

---

[175] John F. Kennedy, Campaign Speech at the Waldorf-Astoria Hotel, New York, 12 October 1960.

The Army, especially, came under questioning since people could not understand why the mightiest army in the world could not whip a small nation into line. The reasons, of course, are listed herein, and they should raise questions.

Many capable and experienced professional officers were rifted, including some of my friends, and often the wrong officers were let go. Morale fell along with appropriations. It took decades to recover.

The domestic upheavals of the war ended the draft and caused the creation of the all-volunteer military. It provides jobs and honorable service for many poor young men and women, but pretty much assures the middle class of safety in case of war. Has this not destroyed the classic place of the citizen soldier, which is a basic tenant of democracy?

The powerful now truly send the powerless to war. James Webb, a VietNam Veteran and our former Senator, said, "We must not be afraid to ask the men of Harvard to stand beside the men of Harlem: same uniform, same obligation, same country." [176]

There is another serious issue related to our all volunteer army. Since the people who serve do so apparently by choice, we don't pay nearly as much attention to casualties as we do when they are our neighbors' children who were drafted into service. In a sense, they chose their life, along with its attendant

---

[176] James Webb. "The Draft: Why the Army Needs It", The Atlantic, 1 April 1980.

risks, so it is on them. Perhaps this makes it easier to go to war. I wonder.

Current wars have dragged on with no good end in site, but the lack of a draft has muted public outcry. This has resulted again in a long-term degradation of our fighting forces – just how much so remains to be seen, but we hear dire warnings from General Officers about the military being over-stretched and over-used - again.

Part XI: So, Now What?

In the Fall of 2014, Jim Todd gave an interesting lecture in the Osher Institute at the University of Virginia series on the '60s. His theme among others was that half of America now sees the government as the problem and not an instrument of the people with which to build a better society.[177] This attitude is partly a legacy of the war and the trauma of the '60s in general.

We have to look at our history and use it to discover ways to work together and not reasons to choose sides or withdraw from public discourse.

I stood up at a public meeting before we went into Iraq and said that it would end like the VietNam War and was soundly booed in a formal, public gathering of over 250 people – in a Convent – and I am a Priest!

These are difficult issues for a democracy to approach, and I am not sure we will ever successfully address them. I would like to be proven wrong.

---

[177] James Todd. "The New Frontier and the Great Society", Lecture for the Osher Institute at the University of Virginia titled, "Remember When? The 60's", 11 November, 2014.

The First Responsibility of Government

It seems to me that the first responsibility of government is not to react to what the future brings, but rather to create a vision of the future and how to get there. This is nowhere more important than in the realm of war and peace. I was heartened by President Obama's speech on 19 June of 2014. He said that we need to ask hard questions before taking military action overseas; and that (at that time) the crisis in Iraq was not basically a military issue, but rather a political one.

The President also said that it is of upmost importance to define what is critical to the national interests of the United States and what is not.

The more recent emergency with the "Islamic State" has shockingly muddied the waters and thrown us back past such a dialogue. Nevertheless, I continually ask myself, "Does violence in such places resolve anything or just create more opportunity for militants to gain prestige, converts, and power?" Such happened in the rise of ISIS.[178] Yet, we have

---

[178] Thomas Ricks, in the closing pages of his work, Fiasco, writes that of all the dark scenarios that he has read about the outcome of the war in Iraq, the worst was one hinted at in a U.S. intelligence study titled, "Mapping the Global Future". In it the National Intelligence Council feared, "The rise of a new pan-Arab caliphate... which could fuel a new generation of terrorists intent on attacking those opposed, whether inside or outside the Muslim world." P. 438.

given our word to stay with the mess we created, so the problem will not go away.

When I got back from VietNam, my dad ran toward me, his face full of concern; grasped my shoulders with his strong, eager hands, and started to ask me something. My mother literally shrieked for him not to mention VietNam - that we were never going to talk about that again. Such was her pain. Dad's face fell; and we never talked about it – ever! Now it is too late.

But you and I must talk about it. Our citizens must not allow a political elite to do all the thinking. We must hold our government accountable; but, first we must be informed, thoughtful, and outspoken. It is not only our right; it is our duty. It is why Mr. Jefferson founded the University of Virginia. I can see Monticello from my mailbox, and think about how he looked with his telescope down at the beginning of construction of that University and hoped he was helping educate the people so they could engage their political process with intelligence and caution.

My first memory of our political process was my mom and dad looking at the front page of the "New York Times" which showed a photograph of the famous scene of President Harry Truman holding up a copy of the "Chicago Tribune" announcing that Thomas E. Dewey had won the presidential election of 1948. That of course was not the case, but it was the widely expected result. Many, especially of the opposite political party and of most people after the labor unrest of previous years of his administration, thought

Truman was a dim farmer from Missouri, and was overshadowed by the popularity (and smile) of President Franklin D. Roosevelt and later by the glamor of President John F. Kennedy and even the smooth-talking Republican Candidate, Thomas E. Dewey

My reading tells me this is just not the case. Truman was one tough cowboy. Five months prior to the election, he toured the country from east to west and back again, ostensibly to receive an honorary doctorate from the University of California at Berkeley and to deliver a speech at their baccalaureate ceremony. The speech was carried across the country by radio, and I think that speech, along with his almost 24,000 mile whistle-stop campaign in September, determined the outcome of the election at the last moment. It was sincere and courageous, and addressed our place in the world and how our humanity needs to stand at the center of public debate and public policy. I quote it here as I approach the end of this study. As you read it, however, think of how such lofty words can also convince us to engage in foreign interventions.

Our policy will continue to be a policy of recovery, reconstruction, prosperity – and peace with freedom and justice. In its furtherance, we gladly join with all those of like purpose.

The only expansion we are interested in is the expansion of human freedom and the wider

enjoyment of the good things of the earth in all countries

The only prize we covet is the respect and good will of our fellow members of the family of nations.

The only realm in which we aspire to eminence exists in the minds of men, where authority is exercised through the qualities of sincerity, compassion, and right conduct...

I believe the men and women of every part of the globe intensely desire peace and freedom. I believe good people everywhere will not permit their rulers, no matter how powerful they may have made themselves, to lead them to destruction. America has faith in people. It knows that rulers rise and fall, but that the people live on.[179]

Asking the Right Questions

When our infant country made a treaty with Prussia in 1785, we agreed to hold sacrosanct in the event of war all women and children, scholars, farmers, artisans, factory workers, fishermen, and inhabitants of unfortified towns. Prisoners of war were to be housed and fed the same as our own troops.[180] This

---

[179] Personal Papers, Harry S Truman. 12 June 1948. as quoted by McCullough, David. <u>Truman</u>. Simon & Schuster, New York, 1992. P. 628.
[180] Caplow and Hicks. P. 55.

attitude regarding warfare did not last long. By the time of WWII, we were carpet-bombing cities in Germany and Japan. Caplow also states that there is no such thing as a large, peaceful state, and there never has been.[181] Taken together, these assertions should cause us alarm.

Our forbearers created a new thing here on this continent – a nation subservient to the people, but if that is to be so, the people need to be involved in the political process. For each of us alive at the time, "everything changed" in the 60's, but at the deeper, cultural level everything seems to have stayed the same. Our decisions made in the past have reaped horrid results. Examples might include trusting the U.S.S.R. to open a land front against Japan with tens of thousands of tanks, trucks, and planes we supplied them, to have them delay until the war was just about over to attack China and turn over the weapons to Mao to use to defeat the pro-western Nationalist Chinese Army and China's legitimate leadership. This betrayal, which should have been anticipated, led directly to the Korean and VietNam Wars. We do things without considering the long term possibilities.

Another, older example might be the French and British establishment of artificial nations in the Middle East and South Asia at the end of WWI. Those decisions are now visiting us with a vengeance. Islamic militants have a long memory. One of those memories involves the mounting of the Crusades by the West a thousand years ago. There is a long

---

[181] *Ibid*. P. 21.

history behind everything that happens, and our leaders, both civil and military, and their advisors need to know that history before making decisions, or we cause far worse consequences down the road.

We began this survey of history and culture with our Foundational Narrative and the pride we share in our being a nation built on the value of the individual human being and his and her liberty and responsibility for self government. We also saw that this attitude does not happen overnight in other cultures. It took over half a millennium for us to get there (from the *Magna Carta* to the Declaration of Independence).

There is also evidence in our heritage from our Founding Fathers that they did not consider our new country trying to get its way by the projection of force around the world. Of course, we did not have the force to project, and the world was a much simpler place. Also, we were somewhat protected by two massive oceans, but there are philosophical concepts contained in many of their letters and speeches that show that they wished us to be a peaceful, participating member of the family of Nations, to wit:

> *Observe good faith and Justice toward all Nations. Cultivate peace and harmony with all.* — George Washington in his farewell address.

> *Peace, commerce, and honest friendship with all nations, entangling alliances with none.*

> -Thomas Jefferson in his 1st Inaugural Address

> *America's glory is not dominion, but liberty. Her march is the march of the mind... Her motto is Freedom, Independence, Peace.*
>
> - John Quincy Adams' speech to the U.S. House of Representatives on Independence Day, 1821.

And, one more quotation from Thomas Jefferson in a letter to his friend James Madison:

> *I hope our wisdom will grow with our power and teach us that the less we use (that power) the greater it will be.*

I fear that the Formational Narrative of the United States has been misused in our lifetime to justify foreign policies that are diametrically the opposite of the philosophy of our Founders and sets up the United States not as a member of the family of nations, but as a country which in times of crisis relinquishes the high ground for short term pragmatic gain, and makes us enemies of half the world. This book tries to make the point that decision makers at whatever level need to care very much for who we think we are and look out one hundred years and more when trying to understand the ramifications of our options; and, in so doing, absolutely must know and respect the cultures and peoples involved. Since looking forward and knowing and respecting other peoples is very difficult, and those cultures are, as is ours, determined by their past, it is all the more crucial that our leaders and especially our electorate who choose them be well aware of the importance of the study of the cultural, political, and economic history of the peoples of this world.

Furthermore, social scientists, such as Samuel Huntington, in, <u>Clash of Civilizations,</u> note the emergence of what they call "supra-national civilizations" which rose in the flux that came about with the end of the Cold War. These are listed as: "Western, Confucian, Islamic, Slavic-Orthodox, Latin American, Japanese, Hindu, and African."[182] This raises huge specters of pan-cultural warfare, possibly world-wide in scope. We really need to pay attention.

I keep a list of the questions arising from these issues and which need to be addressed individually and corporately. A copy has been furnished in the Appendix, along with my reading bibliography and some other things, to assist you in taking the next step. I have also included a glossary of the military terms and jargon used in the war to help with your reading and to help non-military people gain a common language with those who served in order to heal the gap between those groups of citizens. I have also built for you an index at the end of the paper edition of this book.

Addressing these questions in no way diminishes the honor due those who have fallen, have served, serve now, or will serve; but rather, exercising such consideration and caution as I describe is an

---

[182] *Ibid*. P. 29.

important part of caring for our military, for our youth, and for our country.

I ran into an old WWII vet in Sam's Club. I thanked him for his service and we talked for a while. He was wounded on Okinawa and his brother was killed on Saipan. I had the feeling that he had no one with whom he could talk.

As I left, he asked rhetorically, even 69 years 8 months later, "When will humankind learn?" That, in my experience, is the question in some form most asked by combat veterans.

It is also humankind's deepest cultural question.

Appendices

Appendix A
Questions for Consideration and Dialogue

- Who are We? What is our role in the world? Are we really the "Light of the World" or are other cultures of equal value to its people? Could we learn anything from them?

- Can we be charitable and respectful friends to others of different cultures? Can we be perceived as strong and free without foreign intervention?

- What constitutes a critical interest of the United States?

- When do we make war, and who decides? Should a President have the power to send our military in harm's way on his or her own, even subject to later Congressional ratification?

- What constraints should we exercise under the "Just War" concepts? Do we even remember them or do we just exercise our self-will?

- How do we address potential conflict with the rise of "supra-national civilizations".

- How do we make war? Are we really constrained by our culture and our history? If so, what does that say about our ability to respond to world crises and threats to our genuine national interest?

- How might we raise up capable, visionary leaders who understand these things for high political, administrative, and military office?

- How do we organize or train the people who staff our governmental institutions so that they function without internecine conflict and distrust and with appropriate, truthful, and selfless communication?

- How do we defend the citizen's responsibility to defend his or her country and way of life? Does the all-volunteer military cut the feet out from under the citizen's responsibility to defend his or her country? Would a draft with alternative service opportunities but no excuses and the certain use of the reserves be a better model?

- And, lastly, how as a people do we address these and like questions? I am not sure we can. It is probably a slow evolution, but it won't happen without minding our history.

Appendix B
The Geneva Accords of 1954

The terms of the Accords included the following:

- Vietnam was to become an independent nation, formally ending 75 years of French colonialism.

- Vietnam would be temporarily divided for military operations for a period of two years along the 17th parallel. This line was not in any way to be considered a political or territorial boundary".

- Nationwide elections, conducted under international supervision, were scheduled for July 1956. The election result was to determine Vietnam's single leadership.

- During the two-year period, military personnel were to return to their place of origin: Viet Minh soldiers and guerrillas to North Vietnam, French and pro-French troops to South Vietnam. Vietnamese civilians could relocate to either North or South as they chose.

- During the transition period, both North and South Vietnam were not to enter into any foreign military alliances or accept military support.

- Elections were to take place to create one nation within two years.

Note that neither North nor South were invited to Geneva and were not signatories. The United States did not sign, but set up the South East Asia Treaty Organization to attempt to protect Laos and the South.

Appendix C
The Gulf of Tonkin Resolution

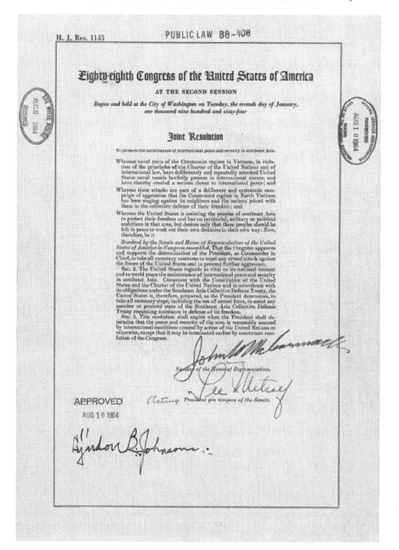

Readable text follows on the next page

The Text of the Gulf of Tonkin Resolution

Eighty-eighth Congress of the United States of America
AT THE SECOND SESSION

Begun and held at the City of Washington on Tuesday, the seventh day of January, one thousand nine hundred and sixty-four

Joint Resolution
To promote the maintenance of international peace and security in southeast Asia.

Whereas naval units of the Communist regime in Vietnam, in violation of the principles of the Charter of the United Nations and of international law, have deliberately and repeatedly attacked United Stated naval vessels lawfully present in international waters, and have thereby created a serious threat to international peace; and

Whereas these attackers are part of deliberate and systematic campaign of aggression that the Communist regime in North Vietnam has been waging against its neighbors and the nations joined with them in the collective defense of their freedom; and

Whereas the United States is assisting the peoples of southeast Asia to protest their freedom and has no territorial, military or political ambitions in that area, but desires only that these people should be left in

226

peace to work out their destinies in their own way: Now, therefore be it

Resolved by the Senate and House of Representatives of the United States of America in Congress assembled, That the Congress approves and supports the determination of the President, as Commander in Chief, to take all necessary measures to repel any armed attack against the forces of the United States and to prevent further aggression.

Section 2. The United States regards as vital to its national interest and to world peace the maintenance of international peace and security in southeast Asia. Consonant with the Constitution of the United States and the Charter of the United Nations and in accordance with its obligations under the Southeast Asia Collective Defense Treaty, the United States is, therefore, prepared, as the President determines, to take all necessary steps, including the use of armed force, to assist any member or protocol state of the Southeast Asia Collective Defense Treaty requesting assistance in defense of its freedom.

Section 3. This resolution shall expire when the President shall determine that the peace and security of the area is reasonably assured by international conditions created by action of the United Nations or otherwise, except that it may be terminated earlier by concurrent resolution of the Congress.

[endorsements]

Note: the Resolution is in the public domain.

Appendix D
Situation in South VietNam in November, 1963

The Diệm coup preceded President Kennedy's assassination by less than a month. Thus, a new leader took the helm in the U.S. at a natural time to reevaluate U.S. policies and U.S.-GVN relations. President Johnson's first policy announcement on the Vietnamese war, contained in NSAM 273 (26 November 1963), only three days after he had assumed the Presidency, was intended primarily to endorse the policies pursued by President Kennedy and to ratify provisional decisions reached in Honolulu just before the assassination. Even in its attempt to direct GVN's efforts toward concentration on the Delta area, NSAM 273 reflected earlier U.S. preferences which had been thwarted or ignored by Diệm. Now was the time, many of the top U.S. policymakers hoped, when convincing U.S. support for the new regime in Saigon might allow GVN to start winning its own war.

Two developments -- in addition to the VC successes, which followed Diệm downfall -- undercut this aura of optimism. First, it was discovered that the situation in SVN had been worse all along than reports had indicated. Examples of misleading reports were soon available in Washington at the highest levels. Second, the hoped-for political stability was never even established before it disintegrated in the Khanh coup in January 1964. By February MACV's year-end report for 1963 was available in Washington. Its gloomy statistics showed downward trends in almost every area.

Included in the MACV assessment was the opinion that military effort could not succeed in the absence of effective political leadership. A special CIA report, forwarded to

Secretary McNamara at about the same time made the opposite point: military victories were needed to nourish the popular attitudes conducive to political stability. Assistant Secretary of State Roger Hilsman--who would shortly leave office after his views were rejected--stressed the need for physical security in the rural areas and the adoption of counter-guerrilla tactics as the preconditions to success. These interesting reversals of nominal functional preferences indicate that there was at least a sufficiently broad awareness within U.S. Officialdom to permit a useful debate on U.S. actions which might deal more successfully with this seamless web of political-military issues. Certainly the intelligence picture was dark enough to prompt such a debate: the SNIE on short-term prospects in Southeast Asia warned that ". . . South Vietnam has, at best, an even chance of withstanding the insurgency menace during the next few weeks or months."

[The Pentagon Papers, Volume 3, Chapter 1, "U.S. Programs in South VietNam. Beacon Press, 1971. P.2.]

Appendix E
The Landing of U.S. Ground Forces

Nothing else was, in fact, working. General Khanh's government was reorganized in November 1964 to give it the appearance of civilian leadership. Khanh finally fell in midFebruary 1965 and was replaced by the Quat regime. Earlier that month the insurgents had attacked the U.S. base at Pleiku, killing eight Americans. Similar attacks late in 1964 had brought about recommendations for reprisal attacks. These had been disapproved because of timing. On this occasion, however, the President approved the FLAMING DART retaliatory measures.

Presidential assistant McGeorge Bundy was in SVN when the Viet Cong attacked the U.S. facilities in Pleiku. He recommended to the President that, in addition to retaliatory measures, the U.S. initiate phase II of the military measures against NVN. The fall of the Khanh regime a week later resurrected the worst U.S. fears of GVN political instability. The decision to bomb north was made, announced on 28 February, and strikes initiated on 2 March. A week later, after a request from Generals Taylor and Westmoreland which was debated little if at all, two battalion landing teams of Marines went ashore at DaNang to assume responsibility for security of the air base there. U.S. ground combat units were in an active theater on the mainland of Asia for the first time since the Korean War. This may not have been the Rubicon of the Johnson administration's Vietnam policy but it was a departure of immeasurable significance. The question was no longer one of whether U.S. units should be deployed to SVN; rather, it was one of how many units should be deployed and for what strategic purposes.

The Army Chief of Staff, General Harold K. Johnson, went to Saigon in mid-March and recommended that bombing restrictions be lifted and that a U.S. division be deployed to SVN for active combat. General Taylor strongly opposed an active combat-as distinct from base security-role for U.S. ground forces. But the President decided on 1 April to expand the bombing, to add an air wing in SVN, and to send two more Marine battalions ashore. These decisions were announced internally on 6 April in NSAM 328.

General Taylor continued to voice strong opposition to a ground combat role for U.S. forces but his voice was drowned out by two developments. First, the air campaign against NVN (ROLLING THUNDER) did not appear to be shaking the DRV's determination. Second, ARVN experienced a series of disastrous defeats in the spring of 1965 which convinced a number of observers that a political-military collapse within GVN was imminent.

[The Pentagon Papers, Volume 3, Chapter 1, "U.S. Programs in South VietNam. Beacon Press, 1971. P.6.]

Glossary of Military Terms
and Slang from the War

This glossary is offered from my own memory mainly to assist people in reading literature of the war era as well as an aid in reading this little book. I hope it also helps to build a common language between those who fought and those who did not. It is important to try.

11-Bravo: Infantry Military Occupational Specialty (MOS)

201 File: Military personnel file

A-Team: Basic ten man team of the U.S. Army Special Forces. These guys operated in remote areas to train, arm, and lead indigenous personnel, mainly Montagnards.

AFVN: Armed Forces Vietnam radio station (ie: Adrian Cronauer's program, "Dawn Buster" - "Good Morning, VietNam!")

Agent Orange: Also agents White, Blue, Purple, and others – defoliants used to limit concealment of enemy troops. It worked well, but at huge cost to the health of personnel of all sides. Very heavy concentrations were used in I Corps, Western III Corps, and parts of the Delta.

AHB: Assault Helicopter Battalion

AID: Agency for International Development

Air America: CIA operated air service throughout S-E Asia

Air Cav: Helicopter assault troops and gunships, usually the 1st Cavalry Division (Airmobile)

Airborne: Parachute troops such as the 82nd and the 101st Airborne

Airburst: Artillery round triggered by timing or proximity so as to detonate in the air and spread shrapnel over a wide area as an anti-personnel technique

AIT: Advanced Individual Training for Enlisted Personnel

AK-47: Main weapon of the Communist Block troops. It is a rugged, fully automatic, reliable assault rifle.

Amtrack: Armored amphibious troop transport used by the Marines.

Ao Dai: Native costume of Vietnamese women with mandarin collar and split skirt, worn over silk pants. The Ao Dai was banned by the North when the South fell, but is making a comeback in the South.

AO: Area of Operations

APC: Armored Personnel Carrier – an amphibious (sort of) tracked vehicle used to transport troops and sometimes used as command vehicles and even mobile 4.2 inch mortar platforms

APO: Army Post Office – in San Francisco, forwarding mail to units in Vietnam

Arc Light: Code name for massive B-52 Bomber strikes along the Cambodian border used to interdict infiltration via the Ho Chi Minh Trail.

Article 15: A form of non-judicial punishment, such as fines and reduction in rank, when a Court Martial is not justified.

Arty: Artillery, ranging from light to medium heavy in VietNam. At PhuLoi we had batteries of 105mm and 155mm howitzers and one battery of combined 8 inch

234

howitzers and 175mm guns, as well as 4.2 inch and 81mm mortar units. We shook the earth.

ARVN: "Army of the Republic of Vietnam" (South VietNam)

AWOL: Absent Without Leave. This is especially serious in a combat area. When it results in missing a plane or ship to VietNam, it was called "Missing Movement" and was punishable by 6 months in prison and then they sent you to VietNam.

Azimuth: A bearing in degrees from north used to navigate or bring artillery or planes to bear on a target.

B Rations: Base camp rations, prepared in field kitchens from food that does not require refrigeration.

Ba: Married woman, like "Mrs."

Baby San: G.I. reference to Vietnamese children

Bac si: Vietnamese for Physician

Bandolier: Canvas belt carrier for clips of ammunition

Basic Load: The authorized basic amount of ammunition allotted a particular unit.

Basic Training: The first level of training for an enlisted person.

Battalion: A military unit composed of a headquarters and three or more companies, batteries, aviation units, etc.

Battery: For artillery units, the equivalent to a company, containing perhaps 6 105 howitzers, 5 155s, two 8 inch howitzers, or 2 175 mm guns.

BDA: Bomb damage assessment

Beaucoup: Frequently used meaning many, much, big, etc – from the French period.

BeeHive: Anti-personnel direct fire artillery round that sends thousands of mini-darts or fletchettes, into the enemy.

Betel nut: Root of the betel palm which is somewhat narcotic and chewed by many Vietnamese. It badly stains teeth.

Bird Dog: Forward Air Controller aircraft, usually an L-19.

Blooker: The M-79 Grenade Launcher – like a big bore (40mm) shotgun firing a grenade out a couple of hundred yards.

BMNT: Beginning Morning Nautical Twilight (Can barely see)

Body Count: A big deal for both sides, both sides exaggerated, but the North even more than we.

Boom-Boom: (don't ask)

Boonies: The jungle, or "bush" - out there.

BOQ: Bachelor Officer Quarters in the states

Bouncing Betty: Antipersonnel mine with two charges, one to jump the mine up to waist level and the other to explode with shrapnel.

Bro: A black Soldier or Marine – Race friction became a problem, especially in rear areas, after Martian Luther King's murder.

BUFF: The B-52 Bomber: Big Ugly Fat F***er (but not to the face of the aircrew)

Bush: The field, away from fortifications.

236

C-Rations: Combat Rations, consisting of disgusting canned meat, canned fruit, coca, 4 cigarettes, and chewing gum.   Sometimes there was a chunk of inedible chocolate in it, so hard as to break your teeth.

C&C: Command and Control, as from a commander

C4: Plastic explosives with a very high burn rate.

Cam on: Thank you

Cao Dai: Strange religious and political sect formed in the 1920's combining Buddhism, Confucianism, and Christianity, with headquarters in TayNinh.

CAP: Civil Action Program – U.S. military personnel working in villages, usually with a Popular Forces platoon.

Care Package: Goodies from home, usually arriving in crumbs, but highly valued none-the-less

Caribou: A U.S. Army, twin engine tactical transport aircraft with STOL capabilities, stolen by the Air Force and then retired. The Caribou had a 93 ft wing span, but could land and take off on dirt in 800 ft.

Casualties: Killed or wounded personnel

CG: Commanding General Officer

Chain of Command: The strict structure of passing down orders or up information

Cham People: Descendants of ancient residents who came from the direction of India

Chao co: Hello or goodby

Charlie: Slang for VC, or Viet Cong "VC" , or "Victor Charlie"

Chi Com: Chinese Communist, or usually a piece of equipment or ammunition made by China to U.S.S.R. design.

Chief of Smoke: The NCO of an artillery battery.

Chieu hoi: "Open arms" program intended to persuade VC to defect to the South. Many became "Kit Carsons" or scouts.

Chinook: A UH-47 Cargo and troop transport helicopter of the Army

Chopper: Helicopter, of which there were many types

Chuck: Black Soldier's or Marine's term for a white one.

CIB: The coveted "Combat Infantry Badge"

CID: Criminal Investigating Division of the Military Police

Claymore: A convex anti-personnel mine, fired electrically, used to discourage the approach of the enemy.

CMH: Congressional Medal of Honor – highest military honor

CO: Commanding Officer, oddly enough also used for "Conscientious Objector".

Cobra: The AH-1G Attack Helicopter, faster, tandem seated, 2 man, gunship variant of the UH-1

Cochin China: The French Colonial name for the south of Vietnam. The mid-section around Hue was Annam, and what we think of as North VietNam was the land of Tonkin. VietNam was rarely one country.

Cock n' Lock: Similar to "lock and load", but on a .45 pistol which had to be cocked before the safety (the lock) could be set.

Commo: Short for Communications, usually by radio or wire laid telephone (sometimes by helicopter across the top of triple canopy jungle.

Company: Usually 3 platoons and a weapons platoon of various machine guns and mortars.

Concealment: Something to hide behind so one can't be seen (as opposed to "Cover" which is something that will actually help)

Concertina: Coiled razor wire for defensive positions

Conex: Corrugated metal shipping crate about 8 ft square.

CONUS: Continental United States

CORDS: Civil Operations and Revolutionary Development Support, coordinated pacification efforts.

Corpsman: Navy medic serving with Marines

COSVN: Clandestine North Vietnamese leaders operating from Cambodia and directing operations in South VietNam.

Counter-Battery: Artillery fire guided to stop the enemy rocket or mortar batteries from firing at us

Court Martial: A court convened by commander to try a Soldier or Marine for an infraction of the UCMJ (a crime). There are three types of courts, depending on the gravity of the offense: Summary, Special, and General.

Cover: Hat; alternatively and more importantly, something to stop incoming projectiles.

CP: Command Post

CQ: Charge of quarters, an enlisted man who tends the quarters at night.

Crew Served Weapons: Weapons not able to be used by a single soldier or marine, such as the M-60 light machine gun used with the bipod, mounted in ground vehicles, or aerial platforms; 60 and 81 mm and 4.2 inch mortars for indirect fire; M-40 and M-105 recoilless rifle for direct fire.

Crispy Critters: See "Napalm"

Crotch: Derogatory term for the Marine Corps, used safely only by Marines.

CS: Tear gas used by the barrel from helicopters.

Cyclo: Three wheeled conveyance with front seat for passengers common in cities

D-Ring: Rings of that shape to hold gear together and on ones person – also the parachute opening handle a paratrooper pulls to open the parachute

Daily Dozen: The 12 morning group exercises in the military, though not in combat areas.

DEROS: Date Estimated Return from Over Seas – the go-home day

Di di (mau): Go away quickly, or better: Haul ass.

Dia Wi: Vietnamese for Captain, or Company Commander

Digger: Australian soldier

Dinki Dau: Vietnamese for crazy, or better, completely nuts

DMZ: Demilitarized Zone established by the 1954 Geneva Accord and immediately violated by the north U.S. Marines and Army Special Forces held a line to the south.

Donut Dollies: Volunteer women flown in to visit troops at posts with music and favors such as that from which their slang name is derived. These visits were rare and were under the USO.

Duce and a ½: A 2 ½ ton truck capable of on and off road use to transport troops or cargo

Dud: A projectile or bomb that does not detonate when it should. This gave the enemy tons of explosives a day.

Dung lai: Vietnamese for "Stop!"

Duster: M-41 tank with twin 40mm canon in place of the normal turret.

Dust off: Medevac helicopters, flown by very brave men.

EDSCA: Effective Date for Strength Accountability

EENT: End Evening Nautical Twilight (when you can't see)

Elephant grass: Tall, razor-edged tropical plant covering parts of VietNam.

Entrenching tool: A small folding field shovel.

EOD: Explosive Ordinance Disposal

ETA: Estimated Time of Arrival

ETS: Estimated Time of Departure

Extraction: To airlift a patrol or unit out of the bush, sometimes under fire, which is then called a "Hot" extraction.

FAC: Forward Air Controller – usually a light plane with more brave men inside.

Fart Sack: Sleeping bag (or so I am told by a Marine friend)

Fast Mover: Jet Fighter.

FDC: Fire Direction Center of an artillery unit

FEBA: Forward Edge of the Battle Area (line of departure)

Field Strip: Disassemble and reassemble a weapon, often in the dark

Field strip: Disassemble, clean, and reassemble a weapon. We had to learn to do it in the dark.

FIGMO: F**k it, I Got My Orders (said by a short timer)

Final Protective Line: Pre-planned interlocking patterns of fire of every weapon available in the event a unit is about to be over run.

Fini: All over, from the French. Sometimes meaning to die.

Fire Base: Base for fire support of forward ground operations

Fire for Effect: Artillery term for continuous firing by all tubes until the target is reduced.

Fire in the Hole: Warning that explosives are about to be detonated

Fire Mission: The request or carrying out of such for artillery fires.

Five by Five: As in "I hear you 5x5", meaning loud and clear

Flack Jacket: Heavy fiberglass–filled vest that would stop most shrapnel, but not bullets

Flare: Illumination projectile that light up the night.

FNG: F**ing New Guy – stay away from him until he learns how to survive and take care of you.

FO: Forward Observer – guy on the ground adjusting artillery fire

Four-Duce: The big mortar, 4.2 inches in bore, and very serious.

Frag: A fragmentation grenade

Fragging: The assassination of an officer by his own men.

Free Fire Zone: Area where no permission from the Vietnamese authorities was required for a fire mission.

Freedom Bird: A jet that takes you home after your tour of duty.

Friendly Fire: Damage done by our own weapons. This is common in any war.

FUBAR: "F**ked Up Beyond All Recognition" – any disorganized operation

Gook: Name used to depersonalize the enemy so the work of killing is more tolerable.

GR Point: Graves Registration

Grenade: They came in several varieties – Explosive Fragmentation, CS gas (rare), thermite for melting through steel (also rare), and signal smoke of several colors used to mark units on the ground for helicopter extraction

Grids: Military maps are broken into grids for easy reference for navigation or fire missions.

Ground Search Radar: Anti-personnel radar used in flat areas to detect movement at night out to about 7 miles.

Grunt: Infantryman – ground pounder – 11 Bravo

Gun, 175mm: A long gun firing over 25 miles with poor accuracy.   The gun tube was 37 ft long and weighed 13,750 lbs or so.   The gun tube had to be changed after 200 rounds, so it was used sparingly.

Gun: A direct fire artillery piece that sends a projectile on a low trajectory at high velocity to the target.

Gunny: Marine Top Sergeant

GVN: Government of South VietNam

H&I: Artillery term for Harass and Interdict – fire on pre-determined locations, often at night, to deny the enemy freedom of movement.

Hamlet: An extended family settlement, several of which might form a village, an official administrative unit.

Hammer & Anvil: Tactic of setting a blocking position and driving the enemy into it.

HE: High Explosive – a type of artillery projectile

Hmong: Laotian hill tribe used by the CIA and Special Forces to harass the NVA.

Ho Chi Minh Trail: A very extensive pattern of trails mostly in Laos and Cambodia used to bring troops and war material south. Construction was begun as early as 1950.

Hoa Hao: Pronounced "Wah Ho", this Buddhist sect in the Mekong Delta was fiercely anti-communist and had a militia.

Hooch Girl: Local woman hired to care for the personal property of U.S. personnel – maid or laundress

Hooch: A hut usually built by the troops

Howard Johnsons: Pushcart vendors.

Howitzer, 105mm: A light, towed howitzer for work up to about 5 miles.

Howitzer, 155mm: A tracked howitzer which was the workhorse of the war, firing about 12 miles with projectiles of about 150 lbs

Howitzer, 8 in: A tracked howitzer capable of firing a 200 lb round 8 miles with pinpoint accuracy.

Howitzer: An indirect fire artillery piece, that is, it fired up into the air and falls down upon its target from high altitudes.

HQ: Headquarters – at whatever level

Huey: The UH-1b slick (troop transport) or gunship – the two blade, turbine driven helicopter that gives the signature sound of the war when its blade tips break the sound barrier. Hueys intended to deliver fire to the ground were called "gunships" – lighter armed troop carriers were "slicks"

Hump: Take a long hike in inhospitable terrain, with heavy pack, weapons, and ammunition.

IG: Inspector General

Immersion Foot: Check your guys' feet daily for rot.

In Country: In VietNam

Incoming: Self explanatory. Clearly, the brain (I am told the Sub-Cortex) learns quickly to distinguish the sounds made by incoming and outgoing artillery, mortar, and rifle rounds, even when asleep.

Increments: Removable charges on mortar fins or artillery bags to adjust range

Indian Country: The area out there beyond our control.

Individual Weapons: Weapons carried by the foot soldier or on the person of any other personnel, such as the M-16 automatic light assault rifle; M-14 rifle, automatic or semi-automatic depending on model M-79 Grenade Launcher; M-1911 .45 Cal Pistol; M-1, M-2, and the M1A1 Carbine Rifles used by ARVN.

Insert: To deploy by helicopter into a tactical area

Iron Triangle: VC dominated area in the CuChi district

It Don't Mean Nothing: Nihilistic saying intended to minimize the horror of death and mayhem

JAG: Judge Advocate General- military lawyers

JP-4: Jet fuel, used in helicopters as well as fighters

Jungle Fatigues: Lightweight tropical battle dress, called Utilities in the USMC

K-Bar: Combat Knife

K, or Klick: one kilometer

Khmer People: Descendants of ancient residents of S.E. Asia

KIA: Killed in Action – either side

Kit Carson: A Chu Hoi scout, that is a VC who came over to the South and worked as a guide.

L-19: Light spotter plane, also known as he "Bird Dog" (I found out that you can't run and hop into one of these with an M-14 rifle – it is simply too long (carried an Ithaca riot gun thereafter.

L: Ambush design with two sided kill zone

Laager: A night defensive perimeter

Lai day: Come here

Lam on: Please

Latrine: In base camp this consisted of a barrel to which diesel fuel was added once a day and burned.

LAWS: M-72, a pre-packaged 66 mm light anti armor or anti bunker rocket

Lie Dog: Sit quietly and concealed to see what is going on nearby before continuing a patrol

Lifer: A (usually derogatory) term for a person who plans to stay in until retirement.

Loach: Light observation helicopter

Lock N Load: Set safety, insert magazine, and chamber a round.

Long Binh Jail: Military stockade on that post where GIs convicted of crimes of up to 6 months punishment were kept in uncomfortable accommodations until returned to their units to serve their tour from the beginning.

LP: Listening post of 2 or 3 men set up outside the perimeter to give early warning to the main body – brave men.

LRRP: Long Range Reconnaissance Patrol - These guys were the real deal.

LSU: Landing Ship Utility, also LSI – Landing Ship Infantry

LT: Nickname for Lieutenant (ELL-TEE)

LZ: Landing Zone for helicopters; a hot LZ was one where you were expected.

MAAG: Military Advisory and Assistance Group – oversaw military aid to France and the South. Replaced in 1961 by MACV

MACV: Military Assistance Command, Vietnam – the main American military command based near Saigon

Mad Minute: Everybody fire at everything in sight on full automatic for a minute to see what happens.

Mama San: Vietnamese woman over the age of interest

Marker: An artillery round fired from which other rounds could be adjusted by an observer

MARS: Military Affiliate Radio Station – Folks could call home through ham radio stations and reverse charge telephone from VietNam. This was possible every couple of months but didn't often work.

Medevac: Medical Evacuation, often by helicopter

Medic: Trained and very brave Corpsmen who render battlefield first aid. One of the two most loved classes in a combat area (the other being the aircraft crews who deliver close air support)

MIA: Missing in Action

Military Regions: I Corps in the north, II Corps in the Central Highlands, III Corps in the populated band from Saigon west; and IV Corps in the marshy south

Million Dollar Wound: A wound that insures going home instead of being treated and returned to your unit

Mini Gun: Canon with 7 rotating barrels firing 133 rounds per second. Three were mounted in the AC-47 (Puff), giving 18,000 rounds per minute with lots of tracer. – Used to protect units at night. They could really plow the ground and were a great psychological weapon.

Montagnard: French term for any indigenous hill tribe in central and northern VietNam. The word means Mountain Man. Special Forces trained and organized units from these tribes to try to stop infiltration by the NVA.

Moose: An Asian mistress

Mortar: A muzzle loading tube that fires projectiles at high angles to rain fire down on an enemy. They come in several sizes.

MOS: Military Occupational Specialty – the training and qualification to do a specific job, such as Infantry, Artillery, Supply, Finance, Personnel, MP, Medic, etc.

MP: Military Police

MPC: Military Payment Certificates, used by the U.S. to limit circulation of U.S. dollars in country.

Mule: Small motorized platform used by Marines to carry supplies, ammunition, casualties, or whatever needed carrying.

Nam: VietNam

Napalm: A mixture of Gasoline and a gelling agent, usually dropped in canisters to burn large areas. It is a fierce, psychological weapon.

NCO: Non-Commissioned officer, i.e. Sergeant

Net: Radio Network to connect units in the chain of command

NLF: National Liberation Front - the political and military organizations of the Viet Cong

Number One: The best, i.e. "You numba one G.I."

Number Ten: The converse of the above

Nung: Tribes of Chinese origin in the Highlands.

Nuoc-Mam: Fermented fish sauce used to add protein to a meal of rice

NVA: North Vietnamese Army, Officially the People's Army of VietNam, or PAVN

OCS: Officer Candidate School – a way the Army made quickly commissioned 2nd Lieutenants – with often poor result

OD: Olive Drab – the color of the Army

Officer of the Guard: Officer responsible for a unit when the commander is not actively present.

P-38: Can opener distributed with C-Rations

P's: Piasters – the basic Vietnamese unit of money, amounting to a bit less than a penny.

Pacification: Taming the inhabitants, generally by moving them form their ancestral homes and giving them lovely new huts to live in behind barbed wire so as to win their hearts and minds.

Papa San: Pidgin for an older Vietnamese man

Pathet Lao: Lao Communists under control of the Vietnamese Communist Party

PAVN: People's Army of VietNam (the North)

PBR: River Patrol Boat of the Brown Water Navy

Perimeter: Outer limits of a military position, usually with fighting holes, barbed wire, and Claymores

PFs: Popular Forces, village men sort of trained and given a rifle to help protect their village. They sustained the highest proportion of casualties in the war.

Phoenix Program: Intelligence based campaign to damage the VC infrastructure by kidnapping or killing cadres.

Phonetic Alphabet: Names given letters that can be understood despite transmission static. (See end.)

Piaster: Basic unit of South Vietnamese currency

Pill: The daily dose of several drugs that were to at least delay malaria until you got home.

Piss Tube: A vertical tube buried in the ground with a grass stopper for urinating when in base camp

Pit Viper: Nasty snake, called a "Two-Stepper", from the idea that that is all the steps you get after being bitten.

Platoon: A unit usually of 3 squads and a weapons squad. the Weapons squad usually contained two machine guns and two 81 mm mortars (in the army) In the Marine Corps, 61 mm mortars were more common.

Point: The lead man of a combat patrol

Poncho: Rain gear, never used for rain, but to protect you from the ground.

POW: Prisoner of War.

PRC-25: Portable radio model 25, an FM Transmitter/Receiver used for short tactical communication, when it worked and the heavy battery was fresh. There was also a PRC-10 for more mobile use.

Province Chief: Vietnamese official governing a province.

Proxy War: In the Cold War, the U.S. and the U.S.S.R., almost by agreement, fought through proxy governments and not directly.

PSP: Pierced Steel Plate, interlocking sheets of steel that are used to form a hardstand or runway.

PTSD: Post Traumatic Stress Disorder caused by trauma. Symptoms can last a lifetime.

Puff (The Magic Dragon): AC-47 Gunship with 3 Gatling guns, each firing 6000 rounds a minute – used to protect perimeters at night.

Punji stick: Sharpened stake, usually bamboo, used in booby traps

Quad Mount: Four M-60 or .50 Cal machine guns, two up and two underneath with one mount,. used in truck beds or on helicopters.

Quantico: Marine training base in Virginia

R&R: Rest and Recreation – a 3 to 7 day break from the war, sometimes in-country and sometimes at places like Hong Kong, Penang, or Thailand

RA: Regular Army – careerist, as opposed to reservists – those signed up for a short term of years

Rack: Cot for sleeping when in base camp, or mythical equipment of round-eyed women.

Rappel: Descend from cliff or helicopter by line.

Ready Reaction Force: Unit on standby with weapons ready and transportation available to respond to other units in trouble.

Recoilless Rifle: The replacement for the old Bazooka rocket launcher. It is a very effective, high velocity chamber-charged weapon that has no recoil because the reaction to the acceleration of the projectile is the mass of the gas expelled out of the breech. This gives hard-hitting, highly accurate firepower without having to have recoil mechanisms and large mass of carriage and tube.

Red Alert: Urgent form of warning signaling an imminent enemy attack, usually a hand-cranked siren.

Redball: Expedited delivery of critical material

Regiment: A unit consisting of a number of battalions

REMF: Rear Echelon Mother F****r. Enough said

Repo Depo: Replacement Depot for personnel, such as Camp LBJ at Long Binh or Tent City Alpha near Tan San Nhut

RF: Regional Forces, local militia in the South

RIF: Reconnaissance in Force, later it came to mean Reduction in Force

Ringknocker: An officer graduate of a military academy, usually trying for advancement

Rock n Roll: Fire on full automatic, or mount up for an operation

ROK: Republic of Korea troops – tough guys.

Rolling Thunder: Bombing of the North

Rome Plow: Bulldozer blade on front of a tank or tracked tractor, used to clear jungle (or villages)

ROTC: Reserve Officers' Training Corps – College military program which was the source of most Army Officers

Round eye: Caucasian woman

Round: One projectile from rifle or artillery

RPG: Communist Rocket Propelled Grenade launcher.

RTO: Radio Telephone Operator – the man who carried and used the radio in the field for a tactical unit.

Rucksack: Backpack issued to infantry

Rules of Engagement: Specific, and every-changing regulations for surface and aerial battles saying what target can be hit, by what, and when.

RVN: Republic of VietNam (the good guys, sort of)

Same-Same: Nothing ever changes.

Sampan: A small Vietnamese boat, often handed down from one generation to another, often as well used to transport the enemy in the waterways of the south of the country

Sapper: A VC or NVA commando often armed with explosives, sometimes firmly affixed to the body.

Satchel Charge: Pack containing explosives placed or thrown (or not) by a Sapper.

Sea Knight: A UH-46, helicopter, smaller than the 47, used by the Marine Corps

Search and Destroy: Large operations, usually by the Army and ARVN designed to sweep an area of the enemy or destroy them (and the area).

SEATO: South East Asia Treaty Organization, to which we were a party, and which required us to go to the aid of South Vietnam and other countries, including Australia.

Shake 'N Bake: A sergeant who attended a short course to get his stripes, similar to OCS for Commissioned Officers

Shaped Charge: An explosive charge with a concave, conical shape that focuses the energy on a small point in order to penetrate bunkers and armor

Shit Burner: Half of a 55 gal drum used as an out-house. Diesel oil was added daily and stirred by some lucky miscreant and the mixture burned. In the south, in dry season the water table was about a foot down, so nothing could be buried.

Short Round: Artillery which lands short of target, sometimes on friendlies personnel (ie, friendly fire)

Short Timer: A man scheduled to go home in the near future. "I am so short I can't see out of my trousers!" Some made a "Short Timers Stick" or Calendar to mark the days until DEROS. Troops tended to get anxious when "Short", and it is true that casualties tended to increase as time to going home decreased. Over 1000 men died on their first day with their units in VietNam; over 1500 died on their last day before going home.

Shrapnel: Fragments of a projectile that wound and kill

Sin Loi: Vietnamese idiom meaning "Sorry about that."

Sit-Rep: Situation Report from the field.

Six: Radio designation of the unit commander ("Actual" in the Marine Corps)

Skating: Goofing off and avoiding work or war

Sky Crane: CH-54, a huge helicopter able to transport heavy equipment

Slant: Derogatory term for an Asian

SLAR: Side Looking Aerial Radar, mounted on aircraft such as the Mohawk to watch for enemy movement at night.

Slick: A UH-1 helicopter used for troop transport. It did have two M-60 machine guns, one in each door – which were always open.

Slope: Another derogatory term for an Asian

SNAFU: Situation Normal – All F****d Up

SOI: Signal Operating Instructions – an ever-changing set of instructions governing radio communications down to the smallest unit.

SOP: Standard Operating procedure

SOS: Chipped beef on toast, or "Shit on a shingle"

Spider Hole: Camouflaged enemy foxhole

Splib: Term originated by Black Marines to identify other Blacks implying superior qualities than the whites.

Squad: Two fire teams of 5 men each, led by a Sergeant

Stand Down: Go non-tactical for rest and refitting.

Starlight Scope: A night scope that effectively allowed night vision by gathering all available light (as from the stars). Larger ones were mounted in towers with bezels to give azimuth for artillery.

STOL: A Short Take Off and Landing aircraft.

Strac: From "Strategic Army Corps", meaning sharp, well trained forces or individuals

Strategic Hamlet: Thousands of guarded hamlets were built into which to transfer the population to "protect" them.

Syrette: Morphine hypodermic, squeezed like a toothpaste tube.

TAC: Tactical Air Strike by Air Force or Naval Aviation.

TET: The Chinese New Year, or, the country-wide offensive mounted in February, 1968, which resulted in total defeat of enemy forces in the south and defeat of the U.S. by misinterpretation of the event by the press and politicians.

The World: A mythical place of round-eyed women, hamburgers, ice cream, and no explosions.

Thermite: A mixture of powdered aluminum and metal oxide which produces great heat to melt through armor.

Thunder Road: Highway #1 along the coast for the whole length of both countries. The name was probably taken from the 1958 movie of the same name starring Robert Mitchum.

TO&E: Table of Organization and Equipment which lists the authorized personnel and equipment for each type of unit

TOC: Tactical Operations Center

Toi yen em nhieu lam: I love you too much (until this afternoon)

TonKin Gulf Incident (Resolution): President Johnson's excuse and authorization for going to war without a Declaration (see following this section)

Top: Usually an E-7 Sergeant serving a Company Command.

TOT: Time on target – a technique developed in WWI wherein various artillery pieces with different trajectories and distances to travel timed their firing so that all projectiles arrived on target at the same time to devastating effect

Tracer: A projectile which gives off smoke and light so fire can be adjusted to hit the target

Trach: A tracheotomy used by Medics to open an airway of a head wound.

Tracks: Tracked vehicles, as opposed to wheeled ones.

Triage: Setting priorities for evacuation or treatment of causalities

Trip flare: Ground flare used to signal enemy presence

Troi oi: A non-specific expression of surprise, like the G.I, "No shit!"

Tunnel Rats: Soldiers who explored enemy tunnels, often mined or snaked

Tunnels of CuChi: The CuChi Massif contained 270 km of tunnels for troops and supplies, only 30 miles from Saigon.

UCMJ: Uniform Code of Military Justice – the system of military justice and Courts Martial, very different from civilian laws and courts.

USMC: United States Marine Corps – Designed as amphibious shock infantry, but misused as an Army light division in VietNam.

USO: United Service Organization, which provided entertainment and diversion to the troops to raise morale (Bob Hope and Donut Dollies)

Viet Cong: Indigenous enemy forces in the south, as opposed to infiltration regular soldiers from the North (NVA)

Viet Minh: "Viet Nam Doc Lap Dong Minh Hoi", established by Ho Chi Minh (or whatever his real name was) in 1941 to end French Colonialism in VietNam. Somehow, we took over when the French were defeated.

Vietnamization: The process of turning over the fighting to the ARVN (sound familiar?)

Village: A Vietnamese Village, an administrative unit with a Village Chief. A Village might consist of several smaller units, called hamlets.

VVA: Vietnam Veterans of America – we had to start our own veterans organization.

Wake-Up: Last day of duty in VietNam. Ie: wake up from a bad dream

Web Gear: Canvas belting and shoulder straps for carrying equipment and ammunition

Weed: Marijuana, widely used late in the war

White Mice: South Vietnamese Police

WIA: Wounded In Action

WP: White Phosphorus – artillery projectile or aerial bomb which makes a violent burst of white smoke and burning phosphorus, used as a marking round for further adjustment of fire. It cannot be extinguished, and if it hits a person, it will continue to burn through. Water will not put it out.

Xin loi: Sorry bout that

XO: Executive Officer of a unit: for a company this would be a First Lieutenant, for a Battalion it would be a Major.

Yard: GI for "Montagnard"

Zap: To kill

Zero Dark Thirty: Really, really early

Zippo Raids: Operations that involved burning down villages (ie. with Zippo lighters).

Zippo: Common brand of lighter carried by GIs. Sometimes used to do Zippo Jobs, or burn huts or fields. GIs often had inscriptions engraved on them. One frequently used phrase was: "We the unwilling, led by the unqualified, to kill the unfortunate, die for the ungrateful." Alternately, a flame thrower.

Bibliography of the Vietnam War
And Related Issues

Ahern, Thomas L, Jr. <u>C.I.A. and the House of Gno: Covert Action in South Vietnam, 1954 – 63</u>. Center for the Study of Intelligence, C.I.A, Washington D.C. 2000.

Allen, George W. <u>None so Blind: A Personal Account of the Intelligence Failure in Vietnam</u>. Ivan, Chicago. 2001

Anderson, David L. <u>Trapped by Success: The Eisenhower Administraton and Vietnam</u>. Columbia University Press, New York. 1991.

Arnett, Peter. <u>Live from the Battlefield: From Vietnam to Baghdad, 35 Years in the World's War Zones</u>. Simon & Schuster, New York, 1994.

Baker, Mark. <u>Nam: The Vietnam War in the Words of the Men and Women Who Fought There</u>. U.S.A: Cooper Square Press, 1981. Paper.

Bao Ninh. <u>The Sorrow of War</u>, Secker and Warburg, London, 1991.

Baritz, Loren. <u>Backfire: A History of How American Culture Led Us Into Vietnam and Made Us Fight the Way We Did</u>. William Morrow, NY, 1885.

Bartholomew-Feis, Dixee R. <u>The O.S.S. and Ho Chi Minh: Unexpected Allies in the War Against Japan</u>. University Press of   Kansas, Lawrene, 2006

Beattie, Keith. The Scar That Binds: American Culture and the Vietnam War. NYU Press, 2000.

Beltrone, Art. "The VietNam Graffiti Project". https://www.youtube.com/watch?v=zDjGRRroPJE, Web.

Bolger, Daniel P. Why We Lost Houghton Mifflin Harcourt. 2014

Burdick, Eugene and Lederer, William J. The Ugly American. W.W. Norton & Company, 1958.

Buttinger, Joseph: Vietnam: A Dragon Embattled. Praeger Press, New York, 1967.

Buzzanco, Robert. "The American Military's Rationale Against the Vietnam War", Political Science Quarterly, 110 No. 4, pp. 559-576.

Cable, James. The Geneva Conference of 1954 on Indochina. Macmillan, London, 1986.

Campbell, Tom. The Old Man's Trail. Naval Institute Press, Annapolis. 1995.

Caplow, Theodore and Hicks, Louis. Systems of War and Peace. University Press of America, New York, 2002.

Caputo, Philip. A Rumor of War. U.S.A. Owl Books, 1977.

Carlos, John. The Vietnam War and American Culture. Columbia University Press, NY 1992.

Caro, Robert A. The Years of Lyndon Johnson in 3 volumes, The Path to Power; Means of Ascent; and

Master of the Senate. Vintage Books, 1990, 1991, & 1993.

Cassidy, Robert M. "Back to the Street without Joy: Counterinsurgency Lessons from Vietnam and Other Small Wars", Journal of the Strategic Studies Institute, United States Department of the Army, Summer 2004.

Catton, Philip E. Diệm Final Failure: Prelude to America's War in Vietnam. University Press of Kansas, Lawrence, 2001

Cooper, Charles. Cheers and Tears: A Marine's Story of Combat in Peace and War. Trafford Publishing, Bloomington, 2006.

Currey, Cecil B. Victory at Any Cost: The Genius of VietNam's Gen. Vo Nguyễn Giap. Potomac Press, Dulles, Va, 2005.

Cushner, Harold S. When Bad Things Happen To Good People. New York: Avon Press, 1983.

Davidson, Phillip B. (Lt. Gen. (retd) Secrets of the VietNam War. Prisidio Press, CA. 1990.

Denson, John V. The Costs of War: America's Pyrrhic Victories. Transaction Publishers, New Brunswick, 1999.

Diamond, Jared. Collapse: How Societies Choose to Fail or Succeed, Penguin Group, 2005.

Duiker, William J. Ho Chi Minh: A Life. Hyperion, New York, 2000.

Fall, Berard B. Street Without Joy: Indochina at War 1946 – 1954. Stackpole Books, Harrisburg, Pa, 1961.

Fall, Bernard. Street Without Joy: The French Debacle in Indochina, (Stackpole Military History Series), 1961

Final Report of The National Commission on Terrorist Attacks Upon the United States. U.S. Government Printing Office, July, 2004.

FitzGerald, Frances. Fire in the Lake: The Vietnamese and the Americans in Vietnam. U.S.A: Back Bay Books, 1972..

Fraser, J. Harbutt, The Cold War Era. Wiley-Blackwell, 202.

Freeland, Richard M. The Truman Doctrine and the Origins of McCarthyism. Alfred A. Knopf, Inc, 1970.

Gates, Robert M. Duty: Memoirs of a Secretary at War, Alfred A Knopf, New York, 2014

Greene, Graham. The Quiet American. Viking Press, New York, 1956.

Griffith, Robert, The Politics of Fear: Joseph R. McCarthy and the Senate. University of Massachusetts Press, 1970.

Hackworth, David H., Colonel and Sherman, Julie. About Face: The Odyssey of an American Warrior. New York: Simon and Schuster, 1989, Print.

Halberstam, David. The Best and the Brightest, Ballantine Books,, 1993.

Halberstam, David. The Best and the Brightest, Random House, New York, 1972.

Hall, Michael K. Crossroads: American Culture and the Vietnam Generation. Rowman and Littlefield, 2005.

Herr, Michael. Dispatches. U.S.A: Random House, 1968.

Herring, George C. America's Longest War: The United States and Vietnam, 1950-1975. McGraw-Hill, New York, 2001.

Hiam, C. Michael, Who the Hell are We Fighting" The Story of Sam and the VietNam Intelligence Wars, Steerforth Press, Hanover, 1994.

Hitz, Frederick. Why Spy? Espionage in an Age of Uncertainty. St. Martin's Griffin Press, June, 2009.

Homer. The Odyssey, Doubleday & Company, New York, 1961.

Hurley, Jennier A. The 1960s. Greenhaven Press, San Diego, 2000.

Joes, Anthony James. America and Guerrilla Warfare, Lexington: University of Kentucky Press, 2000.

Johnson, Tom A. To the Limit: An Air Cav Huey Pilot in Vietnam. Washington, D.C: Potomac Books, 2006.

Junger, Sebastian. "Why Veterans Miss War", T.E.D. Talks, May 2014, video.

Kahi, George McTurrian. <u>Intervention: How America Became Involved in Vietnam</u>. Alfred A. Knopf, New York, 1986.

Karnow, Stanley. *Vietnam:* <u>A History – The First Complete Account of Vietnam at War.</u> New York: The Viking Press, 1983.

Kissinger, Henry. <u>On China</u>, Penguin Books, New York, 2012.

Knight, Emmett F.. <u>First In Vietnam: An Exercise In Excess Of 30 Days</u>, AughorHouse, Bloomington, IN, 2014.

Lembcke, Jerry. <u>The Spitting Image: Myth, Memory, and the Legacy of VietNam</u>. NYU Press, New York, 1998.

Logevall, Fredrik, <u>The Fall of an Empire and the Making of America's Vietnam,</u> Random House, New York, 2012.

Logevall, Fredrik. <u>Choosing War: The Last Chance for Peace and the Escalation of War in Vietnam</u>. University of California Press, Berkeley, 1999.

Macdonald, Heyward H. "Return to Vietnam". <u>https://sites.google.com/site/vietnamreturn/</u>, 2000. Web.

Mahedy, William P. <u>Out of the Night: The Spiritual Journey Of Vietnam Vets.</u> New York: Random House, 1986. Print.

Mangold, Tom, and Penycate, John. <u>The Tunnels of CuChi</u>. U.S.A: Berkley Books, 1985. Paper

Mann, Robert. A Grand Delusion: America's Descent into Vietnam. University of California Press, Berkeley, 1995.

Marlantes, Karl. Matterhorn: A Novel of the Vietnam War. Grove Press, 2011.

Marlantes, Karl. What it is Like to Go to War. Atlantic Monthly Press, New York, 2011.

Mason, Robert. Chickenhawk. U.S.A: Penguin Books, 1983.

McAlister, John T, Jr, and Paul Mus. The Vietnamese and Their Revolution. Harper & Row, New York, 1970.

McAllister, James. "Who Lost Vietnam? Soldiers, Civilians, and U.S. Military Strategy," International Security Journal, v 35, Issue 3, pp. 95-1234.

McChrystal, Stanley. My Share of the Task, Penguin Group, Inc. (U.S.A.) 2013.

McCullough, David. Truman. Simon & Schuster, New York, 1992

McMaster, H.R. Dereliction of Duty: Johnson, McNamara, The Joint Chiefs of Staff and the Lies that Led to Vietnam. Harper Perennial, NY 1997.

Meet the Press, NBC Television Network, Interview with Colin Powell by Chuck Todd, 6 September 2015.

Melville, Herman. White Jacket; or The World in a Man-of-War, Harper and Brothers, March 1850.

Moore, Harold G. We Were Soldiers Once...and Young: Ia Drang – The Battle That Changed the War in Vietnam. U.S.A:Houghton Mifflin, 1992. Print

Morgan, Ted. The Valley of Death: The Tragedy at Dien Bien Phu That Led America Into the Vietnam War. Random House, New York, 2010.

Nagl, John A. Knife Fights: A Memoir of Modern War in Theory and Practice, Penguin Press, 2014.

Ninh, Bao. The Sorrow of War, Hanoi: Writers' Association Publishing House, 1991. Print

O'Brien, Tim. Going After Cacciato, Dell Publishing, New York, 1975.

O'Brien, Tim. The Things They Carried. U.S.A: Houghton Mifflin, 1990.

Page, Tim. Page after Page: Memoirs of a War-Torn Photographer. Athenium, 1989.

Palmer, Bruce, Jr. The 25-Yeaer War: America's Military Role in VietNam. Simon & Schuster, Inc, New York, 1984.

Prados, John. "The Gulf of Tonkin Incident, 40 Years Later", National Security Archive, EBB # 132, 2004.

Prados, John. VietNam: The History of an Unwinnable War, 1945 – 1975. University Press of Kansas, 2009.

Prosser, Michael H. Sow the Wind, Reap the Whirlwind, Volumes I & II, William Morrow & Co., New York. 1970.

Quirk, Robert E. _An Affair of Honor: Woodrow Wilson and the Occupation of Vera Cruz_, New York, McGraw-Hill, 1962.

Race, Jeffrey. _War Comes to Long An: Revolutionary Conflict in a Vietnamese Province_, University of California Press, 1972.

Rand Corporation. "Evolution of a Vietnamese Village", Memorandum RM-4442-1-ARPA. Prepared for the Advanced Research Projects Agency, U.S.A. April, 1965.

Reagle, Kenneth. "No One Calls Me Hero," S.P. Amaon, 2008.

Reppenhagen, Garett. "I Was an American Sniper, and Chris Kyle's War Was Not My War," VoteVets, 21 February, 2015.

Ricks, Thomas E. _Fiasco: The American Military Adventure in Iraq_, Penguin Books, Ltd, London, 2006.

Ricks, Thomas E. _The Generals_, the Penguin Press, NY, 2012.

Rowe, B. _The Vietnam War and American Culture_. Columbia University Press, 1991.

Ruane, Kevin. "Anthony Eden, British Diplomacy, and the Origins of the Geneva Convention of 1954." _Historical Journal_ 37, 1994.

Santayana, George. _Reason in Common Sense, The Life of Reason_ Vol. 1, Dover Publications, 1980.

Sheehan, Neil. A Bright Shining Lie: John Paul Vann and America in Vietnam. New York: Random House, Inc, 1988. Print

Short, Anthony. The Origins of the VietNam War, Longmas Press, London, 1989.

Sorley, Lewis. A better War: The Unexamined Victories and Final Tragedy of America's Last Years in Vietnam. Harvest Publications, April 10, 2007.

Sorley, Lewis. The General Who Lost Vietnam, Houghton Mifflin Harcourt, October 11, 2011.

Spector, Ronald H. Advice and Support: The Early Years of the U.S. Amry in Vietnam, 1941-1960. Center for Military History, Washington, D.C. 1985.

Sun Tzu. The Art of War, Edited: James Clavell. Delacorte Press, New York, 1983.

Taber, Robert. The War of the Flea: Guerrilla Warfare in Theory and Practice, Lyle Stuart, New York, 1965.

Terzani, Tiziano. Giai Phong! The Fall and Liberation of Saigon. St. Martin's Press, 1976.

Thayer, Carlyle. War by Other means: National Liberation and Revolution in Viet Nam, 1954-1960. Allen & Unwin, Sydney, 1989.

Truong Nhu Tang. A Viet Cong Memoir: an Inside Account of the VietNam War and its Aftermath, Vintage Books, New York, 1985.

United States Army Field Manual FM-100-5, "Operations", U.S. Printing Office, 1998.

United States Marine Corps. Small Wars Manual, Department of the Navy, 1940. Also see: "Small Wars", Addendum to the Manual, 2004.

Webb, James. Fields of Fire. New York: Bantam, 2001. Paper.

Wells, Thomas. The War Within: American Battle over Vietnam, University of California Press, 1994.

Whittle, Donna. Vietnam War and American Culture. DeVry University, 2014.

Widmer, Ted. Ark of Liberties: America and the World, Hill and Wang, New York, 2008.

Williams, Tom. Post-Traumatic Stress Disorders: a Handbook for Clinicians. Cincinnati: the Disabled American Veterans, 1987.

Young, Marilyn B. The Vietnam Wars, 1945-1990. HarperCollins, New York, 1991.

Zahn, Randy R. Snake Pilot. Washington, D.C: Brassey's Inc, 2003.

Index

273

274

275

About the Writer

Heyward H. Macdonald was commissioned a Lieutenant of Artillery, United States Army, upon graduation from U.Va in 1964 and served as an Army Ordinance Officer in Vietnam at the forward firebase of the First Infantry Division in 1966 and 1967. He has two Master's Degrees and became a student of the psychology and spirituality of Vietnam Veterans while earning a Doctorate at Virginia Theological Seminary. Dr. Macdonald has worked through the VA to help some veterans of this war come to terms with their issues resulting from their VietNam service.

He was an Episcopal Priest and Educator in Virginia and Maryland for 32 years, and with his older son returned to Vietnam for a month in 1999 to travel throughout the country. He reports that he was stunned to find that he was welcomed by old adversaries literally with open arms.

Dr. Macdonald served the Osher Institute at the University of Virginia for seven years on the board of directors and continues as an instructor and lecturer. He also enjoys teaching as a substitute at the Miller School of Albemarle and lives near Charlottesville with his wife, Sandy.

30584129R00158

Made in the USA
Middletown, DE
01 April 2016